LIFE
ZIPLINE

from Fear to Awe

*To Josh,
my favorite
nephew.
God bless
you.*

*- Your favorite
Uncle
Warwick*

MASTER CERTIFIED LIFE COACH CONTRIBUTORS
GARY CARTER · WARWICK COOPER · ROBIN PIFER · DOUGLAS ROWLEY

THE BOOK ON LIFE COACHING

Published by: Compass Coaching International
                 7777 Churchville Road
                 Brampton Ontario Canada L6Y 0H3

                 www.LifeontheZipline.com

All scripture quotations, unless otherwise indicated, are taken from the HOLY BIBLE, NEW INTERNATIONAL VERSION®. NIV®. Copyright ©1973, 1978, 1984, 2011 by International Bible Society. Used by permission of Zondervan. All rights reserved.

ISBN: 978-1461031284

Preface

This book is a great adventure you can take in your favourite chair. Don't waste your time by just wandering through it! Get fully engaged in the process. You should be starting with some trepidation. You are going to need to get uncomfortable if you are going to make the best of this adventure.

All four of your writers are Master Certified Biblical Life Coach Trainers. Now that is a mouthful, isn't it? It simply means this—we all help people think forward. Counsellors concentrate on what is past and how you will cope with that today. Life Coaches concentrate on today and tomorrow to get their clients moving ahead. That is what we do. We also train others to coach because we have been at this for a while and love to multiply our efforts through other Life Coaches. We aren't interested in much of the current profession of coaching in the sense that many Life Coaches in the secular realm simply have some ideas they came up with or derived from their training. However, as a general rule, they have a complete disregard for the most important element for living. That is the perspective one gains from knowing the Creator as He is clearly introduced to us from the Bible. We love the Book much more than we enjoy some ideas from the hearts of well-intentioned people. We learn from the secular realm and measure it all through the concepts of Scripture. If it doesn't fit we leave it out of our coaching. Therefore, you can expect a lot of encouragement from us to align yourself with God's plan for your life.

Normally a Life Coaching session lasts about an hour and is conducted over the phone. The standard investment you would make for that hour is about $100. And we never run into a client that resents the investment. A fraction of the discussion we have on a personal basis with our clients has been distilled into these pages. Each chapter is worth an hour of coaching if we were to discuss it with you.

Here are some quick tips to help you get that sort of value out of this one book.

1. Take it one piece at a time. You can manage one chapter a day or one every few days if you like. No chapter will take you more than 10 minutes to read.
2. Once you read a chapter you get to ponder it until it is time for the next chapter.
3. Find a friend or mentor to bat the ideas back and forth with.
4. Write notes in the white spaces. Mutilate this book by adding your own markings.

Now, let's go ziplining together!

Contents

G. The Lull

H. The Stall

I. The Thrill

J. The Ride

K. The Awe

A. The Analogy

A.	**The Analogy**	**What a zipline has to do with life.**
B.	The Fear	Exploring the pressures to avoid the jump.
C.	The Changes	Adopting a readiness for something new.
D.	The Start	Finding the place and the team.
E.	The Dream	Visioning a specific life direction.
F.	The Options	Surveying all the possibilities.
G.	The Lull	Recognizing a slow down.
H.	The Stall	Handling the breakdowns.
I.	The Thrill	Experiencing the exhilaration.
J.	The Ride	Taking it as it comes.
K.	The Awe	Watching God in action.

1
Moving Fast

Life is like living on a zipline. Most people can relate to that analogy. The funny thing is everyone sees this analogy a little differently. In fact, if we were to sit down with a dozen people and discuss the subject we could gain new perspectives. Some people have ridden a zipline down a mountain. Perhaps your major experience is zipping across the sand box in a park. Others have watched. Frankly, a few people have no clue what a zipline is!

The concept has been around for one hundred years but has been made popular as an entertainment device more recently. There are many different kinds of ziplines. Some home built jobs are invitations to disaster. Those in public parks are safe but somewhat uninspiring. Others bear the name "Death Slide." Step right up! Someone has a steel cable ready for you. There may be a harness—good idea. You may just have to hang on with your hands—bad idea if you might fall from a height you can't handle. The end of the cable you start on is high. Where you finish is low. The cable sags in the middle but not so much that you won't keep moving until you almost reach the end.

The parallels with life are multiple and diverse. You start. Some day you end. You have to depend on the equipment. You only go in one direction. It all ends quicker than you imagine. You get the idea.

If you like the concept it all sounds exciting. But for most people life is just a scary zipline. Back in the 1800s Henry David Thoreau wrote this famous quote,

> "The mass of men live lives of quiet desperation. What is called resignation is confirmed desperation."

Not exactly upbeat on the ride, wouldn't you agree? He had some other things to say that were rather profound if not tedious. For example, he mused:

> "I went to the woods because I wished to live deliberately, to front only the essential facts of life, and see if I could not learn what it had to teach, and not, when I came to die, discover that I had not lived. I did not wish to live what was not life, living is so dear; nor did I wish to practice resignation, unless it was quite necessary. I wanted to live deep and suck out all the marrow of life, to live so sturdily and Spartan-like as to put to rout all that was not life, to cut a broad swath and shave close, to drive life into a corner, and reduce it to its

lowest terms, and, if it proved to be mean, why then to get the whole and genuine meanness of it, and publish its meanness to the world; or if it were sublime, to know it by experience, and be able to give a true account of it in my next excursion. For most men, it appears to me, are in a strange uncertainty about it, whether it is of the devil or of God, and have somewhat hastily concluded that it is the chief end of man here to 'glorify God and enjoy him forever.'"

We get the struggle. But is it really that difficult? It was obviously tough in the 1800s just like it is today. But really, is that all there is? Muddle around. Fiddle with the ineffective. Experiment with the stimulating. Dangle.

Perhaps the sad part is that he is correct. But many have simply turned up the noise and the visual images so they don't notice.

There is a better way. We are four guys who have found it. Oh, for sure, we have been sideswiped by a few tree branches riding down the zipline so far. We will share some of that with you. (Where there is a distinct personal story we will tell you who is talking.) But there is no doubt to us as four men, who have learned the art and science of life coaching, that we help most of our clients find greater satisfaction, direction and significance on their personal ziplines. A small portion of the patterns and ideas we recommend are included in this book. The danger is that you will just let the questions slip past without actually making the effort to address them. If you were in a relationship with a good Life Coach, your coach would be sure not to let you get away with that. This is just a start. You can get a better ride. And once you make a good beginning here you might even decide to start a relationship with a professionally prepared Life Coach. That will increase your velocity and get you more out of the ride.

You can make no better investment than the payments you make with time, effort and money to build a better personal zipline. You can do it. Don't just let life pass you by. This is a one-way trip—squeeze all you can out of every moment! Read this. Engage your soul. Think. Decide. Act. Then you will up the pace. We promise you that you will feel more alive if you do. And it is probable that you will inspire others to take the ride after you!

Am I willing to suspend my doubts and
seriously consider what these Life Coaches have got to say?

2
Selecting Equipment

I t's not hard to find. Just go to any search engine and look for "zipline equipment." You will find an array of possibilities to satisfy even the most discriminating zipline enthusiast. You will read about uncompromising safety, mechanical redundancy and all sorts of things to build your confidence. Some suppliers are ready to take your money online and ship everything to you within 24 hours. Then the real challenge begins with proper installation.

With the same search engine you can locate "self-help books" and you will find hundreds of thousands of websites. Most of them will promise the perfect self-help book for you. Many of the websites will supply social proof from satisfied customers for whom this resource changed their lives. Now why are you so skeptical? In fact, even though it may be against the law to publish false testimonies, you are not sure that "Charlie from DesMoines" is actually a real person even though his picture is right there.

You might be willing to trust your physical existence to a stainless steel cable but how can you know if the equipment being offered you to fix your soul will get the job done?

Unashamedly we will tell you right up front that all the clues you really need to fix your life flow from the principles and examples taught in the Bible. Everything we write in this book is intended to line up with Scripture. If it doesn't don't follow the advice. But we really would appreciate you letting us know where you think we slipped the wire.

You will find us quoting smart guys like Socrates who said, "The unexamined life is not worth living."

But while he is making a point, you don't want to depend on him. What are we supposed to do? Should we quit selling groceries to the people who are unwilling to examine their lives? I don't think so and neither do you. There is a big difference between being a smart guy with some pithy ideas and being an ordinary inspired guy revealing God's ideas. Therefore, when we quote Scripture take it very seriously. When we quote some songwriter take it under advisement. If you see a name you don't recognize just Google it and you will find information on the person quoted.

The Scriptures themselves give us many timely tips. The best way to make sure you are on the right zipline moving at the suitable pace for you is to saturate your life with the concepts of the Bible. Don't just saturate your brain and do nothing. Let the Word of God stimulate your will so that you will change your way of living. The apostle Paul said,

"For it is not those who hear the law who are righteous in God's sight, but it is those who obey the law who will be declared righteous." (Romans 2:13)

To get it right you must live it out.

Most people think about taking action in some area of their life but all too few act. Health clubs sell monthly memberships with the knowledge that most will not take advantage of what they bought. Most people who purchase any self-help book (including this one) never read more than one chapter. Only about 80% of the people who pay in advance a non-refundable fee of hundreds of dollars for a one-day seminar actually show up.

You are different. You have greater resolve than most people. You are going to be different because you are committed to making a difference. Right? Good. Now all we have to do is help you identify and ride that new zipline.

In the grand scheme of things, your entire life is a one-way trip down a zipline from the moment of your birth until the moment of your death. They are going to put two dates on your grave marker. The year you were born. And the year you died. All that will really matter is that little dashed zipline in between.

On the small scale, every day is a zipline. Today is only going in one direction and can never be rerun. But you knew that. Just make all the right choices going forward. Looking back has limited value.

In the mid-range ziplines, about half the people either dislike or despise their jobs but make no plans to change. About half the married people jump off one zipline and find another. The vast majority of them find their new line no better and perhaps much worse than the first zipline. How does all that happen? Obviously, people need help in making the right choices.

Get the "Life on the Zipline" concept firmly embedded in your consciousness because we are going to give you some really practical help with the ziplines of your life.

If you are ready for a new ride then let's get going and discover the more perfect zipline for you.

Up until now, where have I looked for the best ideas for life?
Am I ready to change where required?

3
Experiencing Satisfaction

Everybody wants a better life. Many people settle with the awareness that life probably isn't going to get much better. Some pick a target for their life and go after it to the exclusion of all other dimensions. Still others wander through life taking shots in the dark hoping that something will work for them.

You will never run short of other people who have a wonderful plan for your life. Some of them simply have a plan for your life that will bring them what they perceive to be a better life for themselves. Others truly have your best interests in mind. Although they may want the best for you, many people will define what is best for you based on what they themselves would like. You have your own set of ideas. But you are also probably aware that you like what you already know much more than you know what you ought to like.

How are you going to make sense of all of this? Are you left entirely on your own to figure it out?

There is no reason for you to believe that you are left on your own. But there is reason for you to grasp that you alone have the power to make choices to improve your life situation. There definitely are ways in which you have been victimized. Your society victimizes you. Perhaps your family of origin victimized you. You can make the list of all the forces that inhibit your freedom about as long as you like. However, while there are many deficiencies in life, you can find the work arounds for a lot of them.

In the orphanage in Pyin Oo Lwin, Myanmar I (Gary) visited, they have over 60 mouths to feed. They are very dependent on well water. But the power grid is inadequate and they only have electricity a few hours a day. They have a gas engine to run the pump as well but fuel is very expensive. The well can only work when there is either electricity or the generator to run it. It isn't easy but they make it work. They built a huge concrete reservoir and fill it as often as they can by running the pump on the cheaper government supplied electricity. They have a red light bulb dangling in a prominent place in the courtyard that lights up when the electricity goes on. Then they know to move the drive belt for the pump from the gasoline motor to the electric motor. For that, they also invented an ingenious contraption. However, since the electricity is often only on in the middle of the night on many days somebody has to stay up to watch for the red light. It is a little inconvenient. But it certainly beats the days when the children had to walk two miles to bring back a bucket of water. And does it occur to you that with no consistent economical source of energy, even the concept of a refrigerator is a lofty dream for them?

The lesson in all of this is that no matter what your difficulties there are probably some work arounds for you too. You just have to go find them. When somebody suggests a work around for you, resist your urge to say, "But you don't understand." Instead try this, "How can I work that out in the light of this factor?" Reorient your thinking to find a better solution rather than a better description of why there are no solutions for you.

The better life you are looking for has an underlying striving based on what you really value. If your life is driven by the desire to be happy you will see everything through that lens. You may mistake pleasure for happiness. Many momentary pleasures won't make you happy except for the moment. Sinful momentary pleasures can leave lifelong scars. A blessed life is a happy life even when others cringe when they look at it.

A blessed life is one where the Holy Spirit personally is the Comforter and where one follows His direction. It is your main job in life to listen for and follow that direction. Put on your WWJD bracelet. What would Jesus do? Now that is an over simplification in many ways because one has to properly study what Jesus did in order to predict what He might do. You can't just make it up. And then even if you have an accurate answer to the question you have to take the action Jesus would take. At the core of the issue is this fact: it is much more important that you worry about how to be holy and let the happy part take care of itself.

You must agree with the premise,

> *"There is a way that seems right to a man, but in the end it leads to death."*
> *(Proverbs 14:12, 16:25)*

Therefore, taking your advice unfiltered from anyone who doesn't know Jesus is a very bad idea.

Without the guidance of God you are going to pick the wrong ziplines every time. On the other side, if you follow His path you are good to go.

> *"Trust in the Lord with all your heart and lean not on your own understanding; in all your ways acknowledge him, and he will make your paths straight." (Proverbs 3:5-6)*

What do I complain about that is in my power to change so I can build a better life? Do I believe God has the best ideas for me and that he will share them with me?

B. The Fear

A.	The Analogy	What a zipline has to do with life.
B.	**The Fear**	**Exploring the pressures to avoid the jump.**
C.	The Changes	Adopting a readiness for something new.
D.	The Start	Finding the place and the team.
E.	The Dream	Visioning a specific life direction.
F.	The Options	Surveying all the possibilities.
G.	The Lull	Recognizing a slow down.
H.	The Stall	Handling the breakdowns.
I.	The Thrill	Experiencing the exhilaration.
J.	The Ride	Taking it as it comes.
K.	The Awe	Watching God in action.

> *"You block your dream when you allow your fear*
> *to grow bigger than your faith." Mary Manin Morrissey*

4
Fearing Fear

Fear is a big deal. Just the thought of trusting a cable and harness that has worked for a thousand people before you might bring acid to your throat. Your brain might be telling you everything will be fine but there is something inside that tells you that you are the exception and that you will die or be maimed. Some people just won't do it; they prefer to take their thrills vicariously. Others say they will do it if someone else goes first. They figure if they are going to ride a zipline they should follow someone just in case. How kind is that? They are willing to dial 911 after the imagined disaster but not be the subject of the paramedics' attention.

In 1933 the Great Depression held its grip. The recently elected President of the United States of America stood before a nation to give his inaugural address. He had to inspire and convey hope for the future. You probably will recognize one key phrase in the middle of this excerpt from Franklin D. Roosevelt's speech. But I want you to listen to the determination in his words. He had a zipline to ride and this was the jump.

> "This is preeminently the time to speak the truth, the whole truth, frankly and boldly. Nor need we shrink from honestly facing conditions in our country today. This great Nation will endure as it has endured, will revive and will prosper. So, first of all, let me assert my firm belief that the only thing we have to fear is fear itself—nameless, unreasoning, unjustified terror which paralyzes needed efforts to convert retreat into advance. In every dark hour of our national life a leadership of frankness and vigor has met with that understanding and support of the people themselves which is essential to victory."

You caught it, right? "The only thing we have to fear is fear itself." Actually, if you analyze it you might say he is overstating his point. But he is making a point at the highest intensity of its impact zone.

Napoleon Hill in his classic, *Think and Grow Rich*, written four years later identified what he called the six basic fears: 1. Poverty 2. Criticism 3. Ill Health 4. Loss of Love 5. Old Age 6. Death.

Now that we have those six named, go and fill out your top ten based on your own fears. You get to add four. You might draw the conclusion that you can't add much that isn't a sub point of these. For example, falling off the zipline would definitely qualify under numbers three and six.

If fear is keeping you on the platform and hanging on without the willingness to jump, what will you do about it? You can ignore it. You can study it. You can analyze it. You can discuss it. You can ask for support. You can imagine the thrill. You can probably think of a number of things to get you ready to jump. But only you can jump. Nobody is going to do it for you. You can't finish something you don't start. This isn't really about the fear; it is about the jump.

The Bible uses the words "fear" and "afraid" over 450 times. That is almost as frequent as "love." In fact, John married the two concepts.

"There is no fear in love. But perfect love drives out fear, because fear has to do with punishment. The one who fears is not made perfect in love."
(1 John 4:18)

When fear is mentioned in the Bible there are three prevalent themes.

Theme #1: Lack of fear of God replaced by other fears
Theme #2: Proper fear of God overcoming other fears
Theme #3: Don't be afraid of the wrong things

All these categories are really important. Several times Jesus addressed the question of fear. He poked the disciples with these questions.

"Why are you so afraid? Do you still have no faith?" (Mark 4:40)

You have to love His directness because it makes you think and compare your fear to something. Isn't that what John did when he asserted there is no fear in love?

This isn't a game of Rock-Scissors-Paper. In that game each object can win or lose. As a kid when I (Gary) learned that they had introduced dynamite into the game I figured it would win every time. I smugly entered the game with my secret arsenal. Then I found out that dynamite didn't always win. If only there had been Wikipedia back in the day to explain the logic to me.

You can invest your time looking for cheap dynamite to break up your fear but it doesn't work that way. Study the Scriptures on the subject and you will find that fear is actually quite impotent when you have enough of the correct character traits in place. Develop the correct character based on a deep commitment to God, His Word and His people and you will wrestle fear to the ground.

What is my worst, perhaps secret, fear that I must overcome?
What character traits do I need to develop?

5
Enduring the Dark Forest

The first words of *The Divine Comedy* by Dante point to a kind of mid-life crisis. What follows is an imaginative journey through the regions of purgatory, hell and heaven highlighting the lives of famous and infamous people. The story isn't read as much these days in school as it was at one time but the truth exposed in such an imaginary journey is as relevant as ever.

Many experience the dark forest in their lives because they finally wake up to the fact they are in a place they never intended to be. As they trace their steps they see clearly how they got to where they are. The decisions they made along the way all contributed to the track they now find themselves on. And the train they are on has its baggage car. As they look around their heart rejects their location as the wrong destination. This isn't where they want to be. Is it too late to back up on the track and make other decisions? How does one do that? Easier said than done.

Some of the decisions we made when we were twenty eliminate options that are no longer available to us now. Some of the relationships we had back then greatly affected the choices we made. Some of the decisions we made seemed small and unimportant at the time but left their consequences. It seemed like a good idea at the time.

It is much like the course set by the pilot of a large jet on its way from New York to London, England. The route is locked in and the plane takes flight. The pilot spends all of his time on the flight trying to keep his plane on course. He pilots his craft through winds that are blowing him off course. He is constantly looking at his instruments to make sure the coordinates are true and line up to his original route. That is his only mandate really—to keep his airship on track. If he would change the course by only a few degrees from the original setting he would miss his destination by hundreds of miles. And if he were to do that it wouldn't at first be obvious. A few degrees difference at the beginning of the trip might go unnoticed. But as the distance increases the mistake would become more obvious. And of course after eight hours were the pilot to look out of his window and see the Kremlin instead of Big Ben, it would be patently obvious.

This is similar to the loss of the straight path Dante was referring to. Without constant mid-course corrections you easily end up in the wrong place. What am I doing in this dark forest? I wasn't planning on being here at this point in my life. How did I get here? How can I get back on track? Where do I want to be?

When things get quiet in your life you are alone with your own thoughts. As long as the adrenaline is rushing day by day you may be able to tell yourself you don't have time to think deeply about the hard questions. But when things get quiet because someone abandons you, you lose a job or your health, the forest can get very dark. There are many other things that can go very wrong for you.

Many of our beliefs are of the "if ... then" construction. "If I am a good boy, then I will get a treat!" "If I work hard then I will get promoted." "If I give my time altruistically then life will be happy for me." The list is endless. But if we do our bit and we don't get the promised result, then what? Can you say, "dark forest"?

How dark is your forest? What light can you see in the distance?

I (Warwick) can look back over a few dark forests in my life. I made a decision to be a Pastor at the age of thirteen. It was right around the time I was turned on to spiritual realities. I was living with my family in Edmonton Alberta. An evangelist came to town and it seemed like the entire city was coming out to hear him. Wes Arum was dynamic and filled with passion. He had a great sense of humour and a tremendous grasp of the English language. I admired everything he said. I gave my life to Christ on the second last night of his meetings and decided I would not only become a Christian, I would also become a Pastor. Things were clear to me then. I didn't know there would be a few dark forests ahead. But for the moment I had found the better path for my life. It was a great start. How could anything go wrong? At that point in life I had no idea there might be a dark forest ahead for me.

We will talk about that later but right now how about you? Do you have a nagging fear that something may not be quite right? Is it possible that you are a few degrees off course?

As we move forward through the book together we invite you to explore your own heart and the elements of your life to see where you can improve. There is no doubt that while the dark forest may come, there is light on the other side when you manage it well.

> *Am I willing to admit to myself what I have been avoiding,*
> *even though I know I must find a solution?*

6
Realizing Lostness

In the 1950s it was always a special treat when schools showed films to elementary school classes. The projector was huge and made a noise as it pulled the hundreds of feet of acetate via sprockets across the path of a very bright light. The image it produced on the screen at the front of the class was magical. The audio blared from the projector and the darkened classroom became a place of amazing adventures.

I (Warwick) grew up in those days. Few of us had televisions in our homes. The occasional child would brag that their father had just bought a television. We would try to get invited over to that kid's house after school. Television programming didn't start until noon. If you turned it on before noon you just watched a test pattern with an Indian's head at its centre.

Most of the films we saw were not stories in the traditional sense. They were films on dental hygiene or instructions on how to take care of your room and wash up properly. We sat there as kids and watched attentively. This was good stuff—stuff we needed to know so we could become better adults.

Perhaps we were too serious. We all knew that the teacher was completely in charge of everything we did. We had better not displease the teacher. We had to listen. This person could flunk us and we would have to stay in that grade for a whole other year. That would be the worst possible thing that could happen.

Some of the things that happened back then seem rather funny in the light of today's fast paced living but we also had something back then that we don't have today. We don't take time to instruct our children on how to navigate this world. There are principles that are in play that will make our kids successful adults and we ignore them to our peril. As a result our kids lose their way, not in a force eight gale but in crossing the street! They haven't paid attention to the inner forces alive in their own hearts and minds.

How do you find your way out of the dark forest if you aren't sure how you got there in the first place? Answer? One step at a time.

Really all this has something to do with values. Values are things that are important to us and they show up in the way we live. Boundaries seem to move over time if we don't watch it. Perhaps you started with high ideals years ago even if you don't go back to the 1950s. Do you remember what those values were? Could you write them out? From a spiritual perspective you have to think through your personal moral values. How are they maintained and even enhanced as you silently slip down your zipline?

Because you are innately a sinner, you have violated your standards from time to time. Those violations are no reason for you to lower the standards. In a highly beloved passage from Isaiah 53, Isaiah reveals compelling facts about the coming Suffering Servant. We know this Suffering Servant of Yahweh to be none other than our Lord Jesus Christ. In that chapter Isaiah, speaking of our relationship with this Suffering Servant says this,

> *"We all, like sheep, have gone astray, each of us has turned to his own way;*
> *and the LORD has laid on him the iniquity of us all." (Isaiah 53:6)*

The fact is there are no exceptions. We have all sinned. And there are equally no exceptions about the forgiveness supplied by the Lord himself. Forgiveness is available. But, much more than that, forgiveness is essential. You can't find your way down the zipline without it. This isn't a book about forgiveness. However, if guilt is wracking your soul with pain you need it—badly. Therefore, you need to get some help. Others have sinned against you and you need to forgive them. That doesn't mean you endorse what they did; it just means that you need to let go of it and leave the consequences in God's hands. Then on the other side, you have sinned against others. You need to get that behind you as well. You might need to take some action on that. Please get some help if you are perplexed about what to do.

One thing is certain. Forgiveness from God is available. John said,

> *"If we confess our sins, he is faithful and just and will forgive us our sins and*
> *purify us from all unrighteousness." (1 John 1:9)*

There are lots of whacky ideas out there in your world. Many of them simply redraw the moral targets to make it simpler to hit a bullseye. This is nothing new. This kind of slippage is common. But you don't have to slip any further. You can hit the reset button. That won't eliminate the sinful choices of the past but it will raise the bar closer to where it should be. Somebody has to do it. Why not you?

Sadly, the society isn't going to help you with this.

How lost can we get before somebody dials spiritual 911?

Where have I dropped my moral standards and need to raise my expectations
of me once again? What has become important to me
that is also the enemy of my best life?

> *"The future is something which everyone reaches*
> *at the rate of 60 minutes an hour,*
> *whatever he does, whoever he is." C. S. Lewis*

7
Respecting Time

One of the many reasons we all like a good mystery or detective novel is easy to explain. We know that the author of the novel or the producer of the movie have already figured out the plot. In fact, they have laboured over the details for months, even years. Every aspect of the plot is made to fit into the structure of the story. The hero or heroine is shown at the beginning in an impossible position working against insurmountable odds. How can the situation be changed? How can the hero make a difference? But by the time we come to the end of the movie or novel it is all fully resolved. Often movie makers will film several endings to their movies and show them to focus groups in order to get the best finish. If the ending is not satisfying people will not attend the movie in droves as the producers want them to. We want our fantasies to have satisfying endings. If the bad guy gets away with it we are not happy campers.

This is true in our lives as well. We lose our job and our sense of peace is severely challenged. We want things to change as soon as possible. It is hard to live in the spaces between jobs or opportunities it seems.

Time seems very elastic and most of us are unaware of how it passes in our lives. I (Warwick) remember waiting for the summer holidays to come when I was in school. The last two weeks of school seemed to drag by. The days were long and filled with yawning gaps of unending repetition. When would our summer holidays begin? What a waste of time! I wanted to go to camp and enjoy the summer. School eventually ended and we all ran out of the doors with unbounded delight. Camp eventually came and that week flew through my life like a bird on the wing. It was here and gone almost in the same moment. Time seems so relative, doesn't it?

It all depends on one's perspective. Conversations are an even better example. When we are talking with someone we love and appreciate we long to spend more time with him or her. There just isn't enough time. But when we are speaking with someone we are struggling with, we wish we could end the conversation and move on. Can you imagine working at the complaint desk of a department store, listening to people complain all day long? Is that a job you would like to have? Some people may indeed like it but there is often a big turnover. Unpleasantness isn't something we value.

So when you find yourself in a dark forest, when time seems to hang in the air, what do you do? The day seems to drag on and no hope appears anywhere on the horizon. What should you do? Stay where you are for the moment. Don't take another step. The first thing you need to understand is where you are.

This will take some work. And you might not be up to doing much work every day. Just remember that the calendar alone isn't going to fix this for you. If you just let time float by you won't have done the heavy thinking you need. Even if all you can do is invest a few minutes every day it will help you find out where you are.

You must not attempt to relieve the boredom or the pain by simply making random choices trying the next thing to see if it works.

Recently I (Gary) heard of a woman in her late thirties who was in the dark forest. She took her last bit of money to buy an air ticket to an exotic island. She didn't have enough money for a hotel or food so she simply planned on sleeping on the beach for two weeks. She left her kids behind. She was recently separated from her husband— well, sort of. She was just going to find herself on the beach on a Caribbean Island. Do you think you might be able to figure out a list of things that could go wrong with this scenario? In the middle of her dark forest she couldn't even see the dangers. She was warned by everyone close to her not to do it. But she knew better. She would be fine. Really. As it turns out she did make it back home okay. But of course, she didn't make any true life progress.

When you are in the dark forest the shadows play tricks on you. Even though time might seem to stand still you need to take care of yourself. Time is not to be wasted nor is it to be rushed. Realize that rushing to the next best thing is not a good plan any more than sitting idly by hoping the next best thing will automatically present itself to you.

So, where are you right now? Do you need to take some time to gain perspective so you won't jump down the wrong zipline?

Am I just recycling the same thoughts or am I making some progress?
Am I listening to the right voices?

C. The Changes

A. The Analogy   What a zipline has to do with life.

B. The Fear   Exploring the pressures to avoid the jump.

C. The Changes   Adopting a readiness for something new.

D. The Start   Finding the place and the team.

E. The Dream   Visioning a specific life direction.

F. The Options   Surveying all the possibilities.

G. The Lull   Recognizing a slow down.

H. The Stall   Handling the breakdowns.

I. The Thrill   Experiencing the exhilaration.

J. The Ride   Taking it as it comes.

K. The Awe   Watching God in action.

> *"Change will not come if we wait for some other person or some other time. We are the ones we've been waiting for. We are the change that we seek." Barack Obama*

8
Avoiding Change

The good news is people can change. The bad news is people generally don't change much. But you are different. You realize that the zipline you have been on isn't getting you anywhere fast. That recognition is the beginning of a new adventure if you are willing to change.

In theory most people are willing to change but in practice it is often another matter. If you keep on doing what you've always done it is most likely that you will get the results you have always been getting. You have watched people bang away at the same problem in the same way that obviously isn't working. Their default option is simply to increase the intensity of the banging. If you laugh at a person banging away you are likely to be the recipient of their ire. You can see that they have lost perspective but they can't see it.

Something in you has to change in order for things to change for you. So let's take a look at how you got to where you are.

It all started with you sensing things in your environment. The cumulative effect of all that experience isn't everything. Otherwise, everyone who experienced similar stimuli to you would respond the same way. Some people fall off the horse and decide they aren't going to get back on. Others try to figure out what went wrong and try again. Some say "Bad horse, get me another one." Others say, "There must be something I am missing."

We take all this cumulative experience and attempt to filter it to create meaning that will help us forecast the future. If you ask for a date with a perfect human specimen and the response is negative you might conclude you are not an equally perfect human specimen. You might seek to interpret your experience by saying over and over, "What is wrong with me?" It makes more sense to concentrate on, "Where can I find out how to become a better me?"

Once you have your tentative conclusion settled you move on to formulating a course of action. How does this work for you? "Since I failed that 101 course I think I should drop out of school and go to the beach." That is an action plan. It might even be a comfortable action plan. For now. Later, not so much.

When you think about it you realize that while these examples aren't from your life you know someone who responded equally poorly. The poor judgment wasn't apparent to them.

It is easier to see it in others than it is in ourselves but many people invest a good portion of their thinking time trying to explain away what has gone wrong. While it might be productive to sort things out in a way that delineates some possible changes to make in oneself it is more comfortable to criticize the other person who seems to be blocking the way. It is fairly easy to explain away a personal failure by saying, "I changed my mind on that." Rather than face the situation head on and try again with some adjustments it is less stressful to just adopt a different route through the maze of possible choices.

Be honest with yourself. You want others to be honest with you so provide yourself the honour of frank appraisal by looking in the mirror. Figure out what is changeable in you that will bring better outcomes. Don't simply point to the changes others should make that would improve your lot in life.

It would be nice if others would also change. It can drive you to distraction when you see someone you care about who simply won't change no matter how much you hint, cajole, nag or even yell. The higher you turn up the volume the more they resist.

You see that lack of change in others but do you notice the same trend in yourself? Do you simply ignore the hints? Do you just assume they are joking when they try to get a message across with humour? Do you notice others repeating the same message to you over and over and find that irritating? Perhaps you even get into heated conversations about one issue or another. How do you respond? Do you just yell louder than the other person so you can win the argument?

You are never going to get others to change. Get over it. You must change first and then perhaps, they will follow your lead. You must be the example. The fuel you burn up justifying your perceived inability or unwillingness to change would be better invested in fixing your own life. It is hard enough to change yourself without minding someone else's business at the same time.

You can change. Do you need to? Then stop avoiding the changes you need and develop a plan. You will be proud of yourself when you do.

Am I looking for an easier way to get the change
I know will take hard work?
Will I name the change I must make and get it out in the open?

9
Choosing Change

Change can be scary and uncomfortable at times. But if choosing modest pain for now will lead to great gain for your total life package you will do well to learn how to make good choices about what to change and when to do it.

A good place to start is to investigate how you are filtering your information. Here is a challenge. Make a list of all the things you have finished this sentence with. "I am no good at _____." Now go back over the list and decide if your life depended on it which ones you could get better at if you decided to put in the work. You might be shocked at the things you could do. In fact, if you are totally transparent with yourself you might notice that the things you are not good at are mostly those you only tried a few times. Of course, there is no point in attempting to get good at everything. But there is a big value in getting good at something else. You can, you know.

So, what should you get better at? It depends on the zipline you intend to ride. And we will help you with deciding that later. But for now, will you accept the premise that you can change if you choose to? All of your interpretations of your experience up until now have flaws. You can learn to think a different story. If you don't think a different story first, you will sound hollow if you simply tell a different story without reframing your thoughts and experiences.

If you are going to get unstuck you have to start with thinking. Thinking is not day dreaming. Most people just float down the river of life believing they are thinking without actually doing more than fantasizing. Fantasy can really play tricks with your zipline if you are not careful.

Musing is important. But it needs to be musing with direction. Reminiscing back to the good old days may bring comforting emotions. The reality is that you have forgotten some of the bad things about those good memories. Those events are not going to replay themselves. Sure, look at the pictures for a bit but don't consume them as your food for tomorrow.

The older you get the more memories you collect. Positive memories. Negative memories. In order to put things in perspective you need to develop a good forgetory to match the acuity of your memory. Paul said,

"But one thing I do: Forgetting what is behind and straining toward what is ahead, I press on toward the goal to win the prize for which God has called me heavenward in Christ Jesus." (Philippians 3:13-14)

In the first part of that chapter Paul tells us about his background. He just says it is all so much crap. Actually, to be more precise he says he had discounted the value of those shares down to the level of manure. The past is real. The past matters. But the past cannot be the sole dictator about your future any more than it was for Paul. Paul had a closet full of T-shirts just like you. Only his closet was fuller. Those T-shirts aren't worth much if you get it right. Paul was able to apply his forgetory to his memories because he had a great big hairy audacious goal he was working on. It was a really, really big prize.

This leads us to the final element in how you get a changed mind. It is all about what motivates you. That is so important we will devote another chapter to it.

Have you thought about your readiness to change? How often do others describe you as stubborn? Why do they think you are stubborn and you just think you are definite? Could it be that your thinking needs to be adjusted so that you can be more open to appropriate change? Or are you simply willing to settle like most people around you? If so, probably you will need to go to the park and enjoy the ride on the kiddie zipline. It will give you the illusion of a big thrill. But no. That is not your choice. You want significance, not just modest stimulation.

What changes do I find to be the most difficult?
What does that tell me about myself that needs to change?

10
Preparing for Change

W hat gets you stoked? Why?

The first question is simpler. The second question is the really significant one.

You need a big why or you won't fly. If all you get excited about is painting your face in the team colours, putting on the jersey and going to the game where you act like an idiot for a few hours you are in trouble. Your team doesn't always win. Have you noticed that? Vince Lombardi was a legend in football. He is alleged to have said, "Winning isn't everything; it is the only thing." He did much better than most. He won about 75% of the time. But then did he really? He died at age 57.

So what motivates you? Actually, a lot of people have worked on that question. Probably the most famous man on human motivation was Abraham Maslow. He drew this pyramid starting with a wide slab at the bottom for Physiological needs. If you have that taken care of then the next narrower slab up gets the focus. It is Safety. Then the slab on top of that is Belonging. After that you get to put the spotlight on the narrower slab, Esteem. The very top slab is Self Actualization. So much for Psych 101. All models are incomplete but that one is useful to help you think about why you do what you do.

Did Maslow miss something? How about this? Don't you think everyone requires stimulation? There isn't much room for that in Maslow's model. But give it some thought. We shrivel up in a dark quiet room and go mad without it. You have heard stories about how people survived solitary confinement in prison. These stories are remarkable because they are so rare. It is possible to control the body from the outside but it is much harder to put chains on the soulish part of humans.

If stimulation is a basic human need then it requires some examination. The world invents artificial stimulators. This is not new. But the acceleration of invention with technology is mind bending. You have to work at it to figure out what is real. You know that. You see illustrations of doctored photos and spectacular special effects that are so realistic in their appeal nobody can tell the difference.

Over stimulation really hurts you if you don't get it under control. Games. Media. Advertising. Sound. Light. Camera. Action.

When we recheck Maslow's hierarchy we recognize that the lower slabs on his pyramid have more to do with a sense of control. Perhaps that's where the zipline trips us up. Once we leave the platform the equipment takes control. You might have some kind of a brake mechanism or perhaps you have a leather glove to simply grab the wire. But you know it. You can't go back. You are committed to a one-way trip down that wire. That is definitely loss of control. Ziplines are really difficult for control freaks. No matter how much you attempt to control life, some things simply are going to go wrong.

That's just like the lyrics from the Crash Test Dummies song *How Does a Duck Know?*

> How does a duck know what direction south is?
> And how to tell his wife from all the other ducks? ...
> When everything seems planned out
> When everything seems nicely planned out
> Well the human race will come and smack your face.

If everyone would cooperate you could just have your own way all the time. You could choose whatever stimulation you feel you need. You could get in touch with the redesigned universe of your dreams. But that isn't going to happen and you know it.

There are plenty of things that are amazingly planned out on the positive side. They bring us comfort, tranquility, order and appreciation of beauty. Prepare to find those life elements and dwell on them.

What is my overall attitude to change?
How realistic have I been about my expectations for life changes?

11
Controlling Change

The zipline of life is going to be a very rough ride for you if you feel the need to control things every time you walk into the room. You need to think about that. Sometimes you simply have to let go of the brake and let the system take you for a nice ride.

The higher parts of Maslow's hierarchy point to our need for a sense of identity. There are two main ways in which we create an identity for ourselves.

First, some things simply happen on the inside. It doesn't always matter what other people think. In the deepest sense we have to believe in our own worth. This isn't some belligerent independent streak driving us to assert our will over our own lives and the lives of others. At some point along the zipline of life you'd better figure out what you want to be when you grow up and then just be that.

Secondly, a part of our own sense of identity is socially constructed. We feel more whole when we belong somewhere and people smile upon us. It might not take that many people to appreciate us to keep us going. Some people find this acceptance in the safe haven of home and family. That is risky business. Events have a way of interrupting family life. Sometimes other family members make choices that hurt. The country song *That's Not My Truck* by Rhett Akins says,

> "That's my girl—my whole world
> But that ain't my truck."

Sometimes events intervene without our participation. Accidents. Ill health. Natural disasters. Even war. Of course social constructs go beyond the family to our community at large, our workplace, our friends, our church, our clubs and teams.

When we are not getting enough stimulation from these internal and external sources we have to find alternatives. More people than you would care to discover that stimulation in evil places. For a few moments in time in the secret place there is a little illicit comfort. It seems to work the first time. That leads to a second time. Eventually the thrill starts to wear off. Then in order to experience the same level of stimulation you find something more extreme. In the end, with the wrong kinds of stimulation you end up trapped in addiction. Secret at first. But as you well know there are many famous people whose secret lives have exploded onto the public scene and we are horrified. If you find yourself seeking steeper more stimulating ziplines for temporary relief, find a mentor. Do it now. Too late is much closer than you think. It is extremely difficult to get out of unproductive stimulation habits without some help.

You will never create a strong self identity with artificial stimulation. Whether you turn to internal fantasies or external fallacies you are picking the wrong zipline.

We, your four writers, all believe with all our hearts that your deepest most satisfying identity will develop as you find your wholeness in your relationship with God through His Son Jesus Christ. You will experience that deep soul satisfaction that only comes when the Holy Spirit of God has perfect reign in your life. This isn't a make-believe religious idea. You will know that when He provides your identity and motivation.

You need to find a great big why for your life. One designed by God himself. This big why will make you cry. There will be a burden to it all. But once you find it you will have the reason and means so you can fly!

Do I have a why for my life that is big enough to make me cry?
What will I try to express my why?

> *"Everyone thinks of changing the world,*
> *but no one thinks of changing himself."* Leo Tolstoy

12
Changing Direction

When I (Warwick) was in my teens I was very active in Scouting. Lord Baden Powell organized Boy Scouts around a series of principles and merit badges. We all participated in the social order because of the adventure of learning about ourselves, our God and the world in which we lived. It was a very Christian organization in its early days in particular.

I remember looking forward to the weekend camporees and summer camps each year. Living in northern Alberta meant more than our share of winter survival hikes across the frozen tundra. We would drive as far north as we could on the one-lane unpaved roads covered with snow, park our vehicles in a farmer's yard and trek off into the vast white landscape with our down-filled sleeping bags, knapsacks filled with rations, maps and compasses. We always started out with unbounded enthusiasm. Man against nature! Although it was more boy against nature. Our intentions were always noble and our only goal was to get to our pre-determined destination and back to our vehicles before sunset on Sunday evening.

We would eat the fish we would catch by digging a hole in the ice and letting our lines down. If we didn't catch any fish we had bannock. That was an old Indian recipe consisting of flour and water mixed together and draped over a stick fastened leisurely over a crackling fire. If we couldn't start a fire by rubbing two sticks together we would use the water proof matches one of the guys was commissioned to bring with his gear to make sure we were safe at all times.

If for some reason those matches were lost and we couldn't start the fire because we couldn't find dry sticks, and we couldn't catch any fish because we lost the hatchet to break a hole in the ice, well, we just sucked it up and headed back to the vehicles early. We could stop by a roadside café on the way back so we wouldn't go home hungry. Ah yes! Those were the days. Friday night to Sunday night and all the adventure a guy could take.

No matter what the mishaps were on those weekend hikes I never remember us arriving late back at our vehicles. We always knew where we were because we carried good maps and a compass. Our Scoutmaster taught us how to use both of these well. He made us see the importance of using our maps and compass by not letting us use them when we went on our first weekend adventure. I remember our first weekend camp out very well.

He took us out on a clear winter's day and talked about how we could use the stars like the sailors of old to navigate our way across the snow. We were miles away from the lights of civilization so the heavens were a lot brighter. We became over confident in our ability to read the heavens after a 30 minute talk. We spent the next two days wandering across frozen lakes and snow drenched forests looking for a place to pitch camp. Tired and hungry, we settled on a place that looked ideal only to find our spruce bough shelters weren't adequate to keep the snowdrifts that blew over us in the middle of the night. We moved several times throughout that first night. We lost sight of the lake and found no ice through which we could catch fish.

Then on the Sunday morning our Scoutmaster brought out the maps and compass. He showed us how to find out where we were. We could see where the lake was, where our vehicles were. We developed an entirely new appreciation for a map. No one ever had to remind us again to bring the map and compass along. We knew it was the most vital part of our equipment.

If you know where you are and know it is not where you want to be you need a change of direction or you need to keep on going further in the same direction. In either case, you can't rely on your intuition, as it was more than likely your intuition that got you lost in the first place. Your intuition was not properly instructed because you went the wrong way or didn't know how far it was to your destination.

To get from where you are to where you need to be you need two things: 1. a change of direction 2. time.

You need a map and compass strategy to compensate for the inaccuracy of your intuition. You will hear it all the time, "Go with your gut!" That is the advice that might get you to try a zipline that leads to disaster. You don't need to guess based on what gives you the biggest buzz. You need to carefully evaluate your current options. This will take work; it won't be easy if the forest is dark. But staying where you are won't get you home. And just continuing to make random choices without complete analysis will likely take you further from where you want to be.

A deliberate change of direction is usually uncomfortable at first. But if you make the right change as supported by proper research you will develop confidence you are on the right track.

> *What are my personal resistance points that keep me from making a deliberate positive change in my life right now?*

D. The Start

A.	The Analogy	What a zipline has to do with life.
B.	The Fear	Exploring the pressures to avoid the jump.
C.	The Changes	Adopting a readiness for something new.
D.	**The Start**	**Finding the place and the team.**
E.	The Dream	Visioning a specific life direction.
F.	The Options	Surveying all the possibilities.
G.	The Lull	Recognizing a slow down.
H.	The Stall	Handling the breakdowns.
I.	The Thrill	Experiencing the exhilaration.
J.	The Ride	Taking it as it comes.
K.	The Awe	Watching God in action.

> *"Like sheep that get lost nibbling away at the grass*
> *because they never look up, we often focus*
> *so much on ourselves and our problems that we get lost."* *Allen Klein*

13
Identifying Your Location

I (Warwick) don't go shopping all that much. It is not one of the things that fill my heart with joy as it does other folk. But I must tell you I really like what most shopping malls do these days. They put up a large Plexiglas board at their main entrance with a complete map of all of the stores that are available for your shopping pleasure. And in order to help you get to one of the stores on the map they usually have a big red dot with a sign that says, "You are here!" and an arrow pointing to the red dot. That is a very helpful tool to help Joe and Jill Shopper. If I know I am "here" and I know the store I want to visit is "there," I can see how to follow the maze from "here" to "there." I walk down that aisle, up that escalator, down that hall and there I am, right where I want to be. What could be simpler than that?

Not everyone takes the time to look at that map however. There are those who could care less about the map. They do not see the shopping mall as a place to hunt. They see the shopping mall as a place to spend their time in aimless wandering and drinking in all the delights the stores have to offer. They go to the mall to spend the day. They will eventually get to the store they want to; but in the mean time they walk by every store they don't want to visit and take a peek inside just in case something catches their eye. Guys like me see the mall as an ancient hunter viewed his terrain. Find the tiger. Kill the tiger. Bag the tiger and head for home. I don't need to visit the baboons or watering hole on the way, thank you very much.

The mall map is just an illustration. Truly finding out where you are, however, isn't as easy as looking on a map. This might take some time—a lot of time. You didn't get to where you are overnight. It took one step at a time. This is obvious. In order to find out where you are you need to be attentive to what is happening in your life right now. Why do you feel lost? Why does it seem so dark? What is going on in your thoughts currently? Why do you feel so disconnected from people you once felt close to? There are answers to all these questions and you need to face the truth about you before you go further. Find the dot and then you are ready for the next step.

Sometimes the truth hurts.

> *"Wounds from a friend can be trusted, but an enemy multiplies kisses."*
> *(Proverbs 27:6)*

Find the people in your life whom you trust. You will probably be able to count them on one hand. You might think of many but cut it back to your top five. You are going to ask these people where they think you are. You want the truth. But when you get the truth you want to be able to handle the truth because you trust their judgment. You don't need doting fans right now. They will multiply kisses to make you feel better.

Ask for an appointment with each of your five most trusted friends. These must be people who know you and your situation. It really helps if these are people who have walked a similar road to your own. You might be surprised to hear them refer to their own experience in a dark forest but that is a side note. Generally, this means that you are looking for those who are ten to fifteen years older than yourself because those are the people you know who are further down the road than you.

Another component you are looking for is friends who have experienced apparent success in the realm you are questioning. For example, if you are struggling in your marriage and secretly thinking about leaving your spouse you don't want to take your advice from someone who took the initiative to walk away from their marriage. If you are looking to get unstuck in your job you don't want to consult with a friend who is also stuck because likely that will just end up in a wallowing session.

Your purpose in having these appointments is not so that you can vent about your situation. You are looking for tips to help you realize how deep in the woods you are and how to get out. Definitely you will need to share about your bewilderment but you want to look for proactive solutions, not just the opportunity to unburden your soul.

If you don't get a better perspective on where you are and how others perceive your life you won't be as productive as you can in identifying the things you need to work on.

You can figure all this out. The Lord has promised to give you direction when you trust in Him. You will find your place and the way forward. Realize the truth of the proverb,

> *"Plans fail for lack of counsel, but with many advisers they succeed."*
> *(Proverbs 15:22)*

Who are my five most trusted advisors?
Am I ready to ask them for some time to help me sort things out?

> *"The main thing is to keep the main thing*
> *the main thing." Steven R. Covey*

14
Sticking to Main Things

What is really important to you is what you value. We speak of values as one's judgments about what matters the most. Actually, sometimes people want others to live by the values they espouse but are not as willing to live by them themselves. For example, some parents actually tell their children, "Do as I say, not as I do." That might work for a while with little children but adolescents won't tolerate the hypocrisy.

We form or accept some of our values because those most important in our lives hold those values. Our parents had values; many of them spilled over into our lives. If our parents worked hard we are more likely to do the same. If they were active in the church or community we will probably be the same as long as we don't perceive that we were neglected because of their over activity. Some have grown up and have chosen to reject parental values.

Some families go out of their way not to pass on their values directly. They want their children to find their own values. This causes problems later on because it is hard to miscommunicate what they really value to those who know them.

You can't hide your true values. Others will see past your words and evaluate by assessing your actions. And besides, speaking about values is a value in itself, is it not? Therefore, if you don't speak up about core values you will confuse people who naturally assume if something is important you would mention it.

The Allport-Vernon Study of Values is one of the earliest, theoretically well-grounded questionnaires measuring personal values on the basis of declared behavioral preferences. It was first published in 1931. It is a psychological tool designed to measure personal preferences of six types of values:

1. Theoretical: Interest in the discovery of truth through reasoning and systematic thinking.
2. Economic: Interest in usefulness and practicality, including the accumulation of wealth.
3. Aesthetic: Interest in beauty, form and artistic harmony.
4. Social: Interest in people and human relationships.

5. Political: Interest in gaining power and influencing other people.
6. Religious: Interest in unity and understanding the cosmos as a whole.

People place different importance on these value types. A high preference for certain values must always be at the expense of the other values. As you look at these categories you will realize that they are all legitimate at some level. But since investing your interest in one or another of these necessitates diminished attention to the other value groupings, you could be missing appropriate balance in your life.

It might be hard to evaluate your personal values in such broad groupings. It is easier to start with the list of values in Appendix A. From this list (both work and personal), select the ten that are most important to you as components of a proper, significant and satisfying way of life. Add any values you can think of to this list.

Now that you have identified ten things that you value highly, imagine that you are only permitted to value five of them. Which five would be on your remaining list?

Next put them in descending order. Which value would you put at the top of the list? Which value comes in as number five? By this process of elimination you have now chosen which of all of these values you regard the most. Assign your personal values to a place in the group of six. Now you can see if one or another of the six groupings stands out stronger than the others. Conflict often arises in marriages, families or partnerships because of the differences in the basic value systems. When one catches your eye as the most important but another catches your partner's concern you must adjust to each other and compensate.

Do some serious thinking here. Are you surprised at your list? Can you look over your life and see how this has shown itself to be true, as you have walked in and out of relationships, in and out of jobs etc.

As you read and study the Bible, can you see where the things you want to give attention to might not be the things that matter to God? What does He want you to value?

Happy is the person who knows what they value the most in life and makes decisions consistent with those values.

Where do you need to adjust your value system and demonstrate that with your interest, time and money? Is there anyone you need to ask for forgiveness about your skewed values?

15
Listening to Friends

Your GPS can figure out where you are down to a few feet because it uses multiple satellites to measure your position. Be like your GPS. When you are lost in a complicated city and ask for directions from someone on the sidewalk you can't always be sure they have it right no matter how sincere they are.

You don't want to rely on one person. You need more than that even though one might give you the strongest signal.

When you sit down with these few good friends tell your story and ask them to reflect with you about your situation. You need their objectivity so you can sort out your options. Listen carefully to what they say without pushing back. Remember you got to where you are on your own steam and it got you lost. Their ideas may seem off the first time you hear them but take notes so you can reflect on the feedback you get. This is not a time for you to sell your friends on how right you are. It is a time for you to find out where you went wrong or at least how you got to where you are.

Don't play tricks on yourself. It is common for people to talk with those they think will give the answers they would find most comfortable. You are looking for more correctness not more comfort. Don't find the friends who will just agree with you or who you can sweet talk into agreeing with you. And don't tell them half the story so they form their judgment without critical information. You can usually manipulate your story and a few friends. Then you can go to your other friends and announce that you have sought counsel and everyone agrees with you. Surprise. Surprise. This is heightened to indisputable levels when you explain that you have spent much time in prayer about this. When you can claim that God is one of the friends you consulted who could disapprove of your choice? Manipulating your path without openness and transparency never works well in the long run.

When you are down, you may be too down on yourself. Good friends will help you gain perspective. Don't make the mistake of replaying the words of a few hurtful statements that have entered your ears. Sometimes things are said that are in no way intended to hurt but given your context they sting because your perspective contains more data than that which one person provides. The individual may not know they are piling on and simply amplifying the pain of other evidence you are dealing with.

When you feel lost you should pray. Pray that God will use others, His Word and circumstances to guide you.

> *"If the LORD delights in a man's way, he makes his steps firm; though he stumble, he will not fall, for the LORD upholds him with his hand."*
> *(Psalm 37:23-24)*

Notice the "if" clause there. The LORD* guarantees guidance if you live a righteous life. But it gets better! Earlier in the same Psalm he says,

> *"Delight yourself in the LORD and he will give you the desires of your heart."*
> *(Psalm 37:4)*

You want out, right? And you want out taking God's route, right? And when you get out you want to be in the best possible place, right? Good! Then just put Him first in every part of your life and you will be good to go sooner than later.

> *Whenever LORD is in all caps it is translating the name Yahweh. Study up on this name for God and you will find He is a covenant making God who intimately cares about your situation.

What do I believe the LORD wants for me and not just for Himself?
How confident am I that if I get this right
He will give me the best outcomes?

16
Going It Alone

Hillary Clinton in her book *It Takes a Village* published in the mid-1990s made a plea for involvement in the education of our children. In it, Clinton presented her vision for the children of America. They can't go it alone. She focussed on the impact individuals and groups outside the family have, for better or worse, on a child's well being, and advocated a society, which meets all of a child's needs.

In my years as a Marriage and Family Therapist I (Warwick) have been constantly shocked at the way we bring up our children. We have fantasized about the nuclear family. The vision most of us were taught about a family includes a picture of a mother, a father and one or two children. You can see them contentedly sitting around the table for three meals a day with mother at one end and father at the other. In fact, we have made that into a picture that we say comes directly from the Bible. I quite frankly don't see it. Instead the picture I see from the Bible is a three generational family (3GF). In many passages you will see three generations involved. The illustration of Abraham, Isaac and Jacob is most memorable. You seldom see only one set of parents bring up a child. There were always grandparents and grandchildren.

Some of our biggest problems come when we try to go it alone. I deal with many folk who are caught in addictive behavior. Addictions can be very powerful. One becomes addicted slowly, one day at a time. It starts in secret and continues in secret until one day a person wakes up and realizes they are caught.

I remember a child evangelist who came to our church. He asked for a volunteer kid to come and sit in a chair in front of everyone in the room. A smart looking confident little boy came and plopped himself down on the chair. The evangelist took out a large spool of black thread and wrapped it around the boy's body once and tied a knot. He asked the little kid if he could break through and stand up. In a second the boy did so and stood up boldly in front of the chair. He then asked him to sit down again. He began to wrap the thread around and around the little boy's arms and chest tying him to the back of the chair as he told a story. After some minutes we were all entranced in the story. He finished wrapping his prey. He tied a knot in the thread and he asked the boy to stand. This time the boy struggled long and hard but he was unable to break through. We all understood. He had no trouble breaking through one thread but there was a certain strength in adding all those threads together.

We can normally break away from a one-time bad choice. It wouldn't be a habit if we only did it once. But the repetition makes it impossible to break through. The evangelist came to the rescue, brought out a pair of scissors and our hero was set free in plain sight of us all. He couldn't do it by himself. But with the help of another he could be set free.

There are two big lessons here. The first one is simply don't keep repeating negative or sinful behaviors that ultimately will bind you. You may be quite sure that Satan will use circumstances to bring continual temptation before you. The illusion is that you just need to do it one more time to get it out of your system. Oh no. When you do it one more time you are much more likely to embed it into your system.

The second lesson is that you need your village. Surround yourself with the right kind of people. Make it your pattern to initiate friendships with people who are better than yourself in some way. You will become like the people you spend time with. If you want to be a grouch find some grouchy people down at the coffee shop and develop some more subjects to complain about. But if you want to make a positive difference find some action oriented people who do good things. You will find yourself doing good with them.

Identify the times when you are most vulnerable and prearrange your schedule to take those times to enhance your relationships with others. It may be that you simply need to volunteer to help other people do something. Or you could create a pattern of conducting positive telephone conversations at times when things are roughest. You will find that your best life will make itself known when you give of yourself to others. That really greases the zipline!

Don't invest too much time complaining about how bad other people are. Just become a greater example of the exact opposite of those negative characteristics. Your world needs you. If you can't find a friend, be a friend. If you can't find someone to befriend, for goodness sake, look harder.

Who do I trust with my biggest struggles?
Who entrusts their biggest struggles to me?

"Every kid needs a mentor.
Everybody needs a mentor." Donovan Bailey

17
Needing a Mentor

E ric Bazilian is recognized internationally as a songwriter, session musician, arranger, and producer for numerous artists. In 1995, he played all those roles for Joan Osborne's debut album Relish, which was nominated for six Grammy Awards.

One of Us has since been covered by many artists throughout the world. These words have hit a chord in human hearts.

> If God had a name, what would it be?
> And would you call it to his face?
> If you were faced with him in all his glory?
> What would you ask if you had just one question?
> And yeah yeah God is great
> yeah yeah God is good?
> yeah yeah yeah yeah yeah
> What if God was one of us?
> Just a slob like one of us?
> Just a stranger on the bus?
> Trying to make his way home?
> If God had a face what would it look like?
> And would you want to see if seeing meant
> that you would have to believe in things like heaven
> and in Jesus and the saints and all the prophets?
> What if God was one of us?
> Just a slob like one of us?
> Just a stranger on the bus?
> Trying to make his way home?
> He's trying to make his way home?
> Back up to heaven all alone?
> Nobody calling on the phone?
> Except for the pope maybe in Rome?

Christianity is not about deciding who we want to be and what makes us happy; it is about receiving the gift of freedom offered only in Christ; it is about learning who we are and how to find not just happiness but fulfillment in relating to God and to one another. There are many religions in our world that point to hidden paths with eternal mysteries and unseen codes and unfathomable ways. The way of Christ is a path walked in the light with other pilgrims. Community has always been at the heart of the Christian Gospel. The whole idea of spiritual mentors, life coaches, spiritual directors, disciplers etc. has long been part of the Christian world. The idea that we have to all individually discover God's truth on our own is foreign to the Bible. Jesus is the truth. We are living in a day in which the church worldwide is discovering these old truths.

You don't need "a slob like one of us" or "a stranger on the bus" to help you down the road of life. You don't need someone with whom you share the same failures to mourn over.

Here is a short list of characteristics you need in a mentor.

1.   A person who knows the Lord and the Book and lives it out.
2.   A person you can look up to.
3.   A person about ten years further down the road than you.
4.   A person who has humbly worked through some failures and come out the other side better for it.
5.   A person who knows joy and peace.
6.   A person who has known suffering.
7.   A person who will listen to you with their ears, eyes and heart.
8.   A person who won't take any nonsense from you.
9.   A person who will invest time in you and give you much more than they take.
10. A person who expects you to pass on the good parts you gain to multiple other persons.

Go ahead, expand the list of characteristics for your personal situation. You can think of other desirable characteristics.

Many lament the fact that they grew up and remain more or less mentorless. The key issue here is that if a mentor has not found you, you still have the opportunity to go and find that mentor. Many worthy candidates know how unworthy they are because they know the short-comings on their insides. Often they simply need a nudge from someone who is open to their input. You are the one who must take the initiative and ask the right questions until you find your match.

Who do I look up to as my primary mentor? Do I need to expand my horizons and find an additional person who can help me grow and maintain perspective?

18
Finding a Mentor

The fact that you are reading this book exposes the fact that you are convinced you need some help. Where do you look for a mentor? The dictionary defines mentor as "a wise and trusted counsellor or teacher, an influential senior sponsor or supporter." Where are these people?

You are not likely to run into more than a handful of people in your lifetime who are of the quality you need for your mentor. But you are likely to be in close proximity to a few. In the ideal your mentor will find you and tap you on the shoulder. Paul instructed Timothy to take the initiative to find people to work with.

"The things you have heard me say in the presence of many witnesses, teach to faithful mean who will be able to teach others also." (2 Timothy 2:2)

Paul selected a chosen few like Timothy with the expectation Timothy would be like him and find a few. The initiative was from the top down. But you could also anticipate that the ones Timothy should work with were also looking for someone to show them personal leadership. Don't let it throw you off track that there aren't many out there you are willing to follow. You just need one and that one just needs a few at a time.

Begin looking in your circle of friends. Who do you go to if you have a problem? Is this person someone you can trust when you need to share your private problems? Perhaps you have never gone to them but when you think about it you realize you would look to that person if you were predisposed to going to anyone. The first place to look is in your pre-existing relationships.

A second alternative is to ask others who they would recommend you go to. Someone at your church may know just the right person for you. Schools and seminaries are teaching and equipping mentors and spiritual directors. Even older people are eager to come along side young folks who earnestly want to spend time with them to talk about life's meaning.

The mentor you need is willing to invest time in you and is able to do so by virtue of current availability. You could develop a relationship with someone from a distance but it will prove more useful if they are close at hand so that you can do things together.

You will benefit greatly from the opportunity to watch how your mentor behaves in various contexts as well as to listen to what they have to say.

Think for a moment about travel time. In the New Testament days Jesus walked the roads with His companions by His side. Paul walked even farther with his companions. Of course, sometimes they rode a cart but the animal pulling that cart didn't travel fast. When they were on a boat they did a lot of waiting around. These weren't formal hours in a classroom; these were people talking together hours on end, as they traveled. Perhaps you have commuting time in which you can have conversations. Take a mentor with you day by day on your way to work.

You don't want to follow someone who is watching from a distance; you want someone right there with you. If the person has withdrawn from active involvement it is not a good example. Often withdrawal from active involvement is a sign that the person has not handled the bruises well. Some would rather sit back and tell others how to live based on their experience but don't back that up with a life of continued service. Your mentor will be a jug to you as a mug. You won't put your hand over your mug but will invite your mentor to fill your mug from their jug. To have a full jug will require your mentor to be further down the road than you but not so far that you can't relate. If you have young children, their children are probably older but not so far ahead that you can't imagine being there soon. You need to be able to watch how your mentor handles a house full of teenagers because your turn is coming.

Most importantly, you need a mentor who loves Jesus, is saturated with the Word of God and has Godly character. As you observe the life of your mentor you want to see that this person is not hypocritical. You don't require a leader who looks the part in public but has private besetting sins that would destroy their reputation if people only knew. You need a mentor who follows Christ so that you can better learn how to follow Him yourself.

Now you are ready to pray that person into your life. You might already have a short list in mind. There is a good possibility that mentor is looking for you already. It could be someone you know but it could also be a new friend.

That person is out there. If that mentor hasn't found you then diligently search for him or her. Start the conversation. Meet once. See where it goes from there. This could make all the difference for you.

Once I find my mentor, how will I assure that we have regular enough contact? What patterns will we set with each other to build our own relational traditions?

E. The Dream

A.	The Analogy	What a zipline has to do with life.
B.	The Fear	Exploring the pressures to avoid the jump.
C.	The Changes	Adopting a readiness for something new.
D.	The Start	Finding the place and the team.
E.	**The Dream**	**Visioning a specific life direction.**
F.	The Options	Surveying all the possibilities.
G.	The Lull	Recognizing a slow down.
H.	The Stall	Handling the breakdowns.
I.	The Thrill	Experiencing the exhilaration.
J.	The Ride	Taking it as it comes.
K.	The Awe	Watching God in action.

"If a problem cannot be solved, enlarge it." Dwight D. Eisenhower

19
Seeing More

When I (Warwick) made a commitment to become a Pastor I had no idea what that meant. At the time I had never even had a discussion with a Pastor, let alone understood what a Pastor did in his week. It was the only thing I felt I wanted to do. I didn't even know I needed any training. It was such a heavy conviction in my life that I should become a Pastor. To this day, if you asked any of my siblings they would tell you that it was the only thing I ever wanted to do in my life—become a Pastor.

I read my Bible faithfully. I attended church every single Sunday. I did anything and everything they would let me do in church. There was nothing I didn't do. I was the kind of guy any Pastor would like in their church. I was willing and growing. I never said "no" to any assignment or challenge. I went off to Bible college after high school. I served in Asia as a missionary. I had a couple of great church experiences serving as a Senior Pastor in Ontario and Manitoba.

And then I found myself in a dark forest. The church I had pastored for over seven years was going through some struggles. I found myself on the outside looking in, deserted, lonely and without any means of making a living. The church leadership felt I was moving too fast and wanted to part ways with me.

So what was I to do now? I had felt called to be a Pastor (with a capital "P") all my life. I loved pastoring (with a lower case "p") people. It seemed natural for me. When a Pastor leaves his church he leaves his job, his friends, his community. I had no one to talk with. I felt absolutely alone. The forest seemed so dark. I sat in stillness, talking and praying with my wife and family. I began to look back over my life. I questioned my calling.

Could I have been wrong about that? Perhaps I wasn't called to be a Pastor after all. No, that can't be. I loved being a Pastor. It was then that I realized something that I had never thought of before. It was a subtle difference but an important one. I believe God did call me to pastor (a verb) not necessarily to be a Pastor (a noun). While it may seem natural for a Pastor to pastor, Pastors aren't the only people who can pastor others. The root meaning is that pastors are shepherds. They take care of sheep. They bring comfort, encouragement, teaching, correction, instruction etc.

I began to notice that there were a lot of people who had done that in my life and they weren't officially Pastors. But they were functionally shepherding other people. That was when it struck me. My calling was not to be a Pastor. It was to pastor. I didn't have to be a Pastor in order to pastor others. I could pastor people no matter what I did. The position was irrelevant. If I worked at the post office I could pastor people. If I worked as a counsellor I could pastor people. My calling was not my job. God gave me a disposition to care for others. I never feel as satisfied as when I am caring spiritually for others. That excites me. It energizes me to listen to others, to point them in directions that are good for their soul.

As you approach your new zipline run, do everything you can to detach the things that belong to your core identity in life from your circumstances. For men it is stereotypically but often true that they attach their identity to their occupation or vocation. Naturally, they tie their occupation in life to the activities for which they get paid.

However, there is more to the word occupation. Think of the word occupation in terms of the thing that engages you the most. That could be a part of your job but it might be something outside of your job. It could be that there is no source of pay for the part of your identity that is your calling. You need to get paid for something, of course, and perhaps over time you can turn the positive obsession of your life into pay. The first step in that direction is to examine whether or not you need to disengage the concept of your calling from the obvious or hopeful place where you might get paid for pursuing that calling.

Once you take the step of dreaming about doing what you need to do regardless of what you get paid for you may be surprised at how much more you can see.

> *What ties me to inadequate definitions of my life?*
> *What are some of the expanded possibilities I could,*
> *and perhaps should, explore?*

> *"I'll be more enthusiastic about encouraging thinking outside the box when there's evidence of any thinking going on inside it."* **Terry Prachett**

20
Thinking Broader

To find the broad theme that can energize you and point you in a new direction there are three things to think about.

You ought to wonder if there is a better way. When frustration rises because things aren't working out always look for a more effective solution.

You might wonder if there is a better place. Just bear in mind that anyone can imagine the ideal place where everything works out. But you need to be realistic about whether or not that place even exists in reality.

You must wonder if there is a better you. There is always the potential for you to improve along the road. Sometimes you get better in a better place. Sometimes you get better when you find a better way. But you always get better when you get better.

Memorize these three phrases and think about them.

1. Better Way
2. Better Place
3. Better Me

You definitely need the third point and that is the one you can control the most.

It is always helpful to talk these three themes through with people who share your values and know you well enough to provide their perspective. On the one hand, you are tuned to see the barriers more clearly than anyone else and a wise counsellor might be the one who helps you to see the better way. Sometimes it just takes a small detour to work things out. One of the keys here is to make sure you are using constructive vocabulary. Your situation could be described as a problem but it contains the seeds of an opportunity.

In his concession speech after losing his battle for the American Presidency, Al Gore quoted his father who said,

> "No matter how hard the loss, defeat might serve as well as victory to shape the soul and let the glory out."

The perplexity of defeat is in itself a wonderful tool if it is used correctly. In this difficult emotional moment a Presidential candidate who lost by a hair's breadth found perspective in the words of his father who, no doubt, had experienced his own set of defeats in life.

The damage of failure at one time in your life will leave its scars. However, there is yet much for you to accomplish if you manage those scars properly. There may be great victories ahead. And if you don't manage things with wisdom you could fall into even greater defeat if you are not careful.

Always take the long view and feast on wider vistas before you take a jump. Pretend you are looking back from five or ten years in the future and assess the impact of the options you are considering. The first thing you might notice from that perspective is that the current pain you are experiencing won't matter as much then. But if you want to get the truly big picture, pretend you are looking back from eternity. Eternity's values are what you must cherish most if you are to have the best zipline ride through your time on earth.

Sometimes people describe this approach as "thinking outside the box." That concept scares people. If it scares you, think in terms of "thinking in a different part of a bigger box." When your scope is too narrow you will definitely run the risk of missing something that can expand your field of view.

Never let the agony of defeat rob you of the inner quest for the exhilaration of victory. Keep exploring. Keep asking. Keep learning. Keep looking. Keep thinking. There may be something just around the next bend. You also know there may be nothing around the next bend but another defeat. It won't lessen the pending defeat if you try not to make that next turn. When you stand still something will sneak up on you from behind and run you over anyway. You may as well keep moving forward. When you keep moving forward you open yourself up to something really, really good just around that next bend in the road.

Who can help me get a bigger picture? When will I ask that person for their perspective? What am I waiting for? Why wouldn't I ask today?

> *"While we have the gift of life, it seems to me the only tragedy is to allow part of us to die—whether it is our spirit, our creativity or our glorious uniqueness." Gilda Radner*

21

Appreciating Your Uniqueness

The word "gifted" gets thrown around in a lot of different contexts. We hear of gifted athletes, gifted children, gifted scientists and gifted musicians. If we are not careful that can lead us to the belief that if we are not in the top 0.5 percentile we are simply not gifted or in other words we are ordinary. The other factor we often leave out of the equation is that the people who make it to the top of any field may not be so gifted as they are dedicated. They put in the hard work.

In his fascinating book *Outliers*, Malcolm Gladwell develops the theory of 10,000 hours. He suggests that the people who are exceptional are those who invested 10,000 hours earlier than the rest of us in whatever it is they became noted for. People who are known to be great may not be so gifted; they just didn't give up like so many others who started at the same time with the same opportunity. The conclusion is that you have to put in your 10,000 hours at something if you want to get really good at it.

Every individual has a one-of-a-kind perspective. It is not so much that people are particularly special as it is they are unique. This may on the surface sound like quibbling over words but it is not. Unique means having no known like or equal. To say that every individual is unique is to say simply that they are one of a kind. But when you say someone is special it implies that in some way they are a cut above the norm. You are unique but you may not be so special.

How we have been gifted is closely associated with our values. It seems that God knows how to put us together in just such a way that our nature assists us to better appreciate what we value.

If there is one thing that my family agrees on it is this—I (Warwick) have inherited my father's sense of humour. I will always remember the way my dad kept the attention of many an audience by his story telling. He was born an Englishman and left home in his late teens, travelled to Africa and soon found himself running a palm oil plantation in Nigeria during WWII and for years afterward. In those early days he was responsible for things for which he had no training or experience. But he had a spirit of adventure and a can-do attitude that took him places angels fear to tread. His sense of humour and dry British wit got him out of socially awkward places and life threatening situations.

You can't get a sense of humour out of a book or a university course. You either have one or you don't. If you have one, accept it and enjoy it.

I remember going through a period in my life when I tried to stifle my sense of humour. I was responding to those who said they found me to be shallow and insincere because by nature I was always the first to make a flippant comment or a shallow observation. Others chalked this up to shallowness. I accepted their criticism. Three university degrees later people were still calling me shallow. But, hold on. I am not shallow. I have done some serious study and have thrived academically. So why do they still call me shallow? Because my edit button doesn't get a lot of use. I naturally see the funny side of things. In my desire to please I had tried to be someone I am not.

Before you take a plunge, do the work of self-discovery. Paul addresses the Roman faith community on the matter of experiencing God's will.

> *"Therefore, I urge you, brothers and sisters, in view of God's mercy, to offer your bodies as a living sacrifice, holy and pleasing to God—this is your true and proper worship. Do not conform to the pattern of this world, but be transformed by the renewing of your mind. Then you will be able to test and approve what God's will is—his good, pleasing and perfect will. For by the grace given me I say to every one of you: Do not think of yourself more highly than you ought, but rather think of yourself with sober judgment, in accordance with the faith God has distributed to each of you."*
> *(Romans 12:1-3)*

Here is one question you could ask yourself, "How has God uniquely wired me?" Paul wrote to the believers in Philippi who were looking for God's plan,

> *"For it is God who works in you to will and to act according to his good purpose." (Philippians 2:13)*

Are you gifted? Or are you just weird? Sometimes people around you can't tell the difference. They take a look at something you do or say and it doesn't fit their way of thinking so they simply describe it as weird. Take that as a clue not an insult. It might be a clue that points in the direction of your uniqueness. And if you haven't explored all the elements of that uniqueness you can have some fun with it. In your quiet hours think about what it is that hides behind that so-called weirdness that could be linked to your giftedness.

The sum total of everything that got you to where you are is very different than everyone else's cumulative stuff. Since you are one-of-a-kind, own up to it and live it out!

> *What can I bring to the table that it appears nobody else can?*
> *What extra perspective, experience, knowledge*
> *or ability do others need from me?*

22
Getting Animated

Here is another personal question worth exploring. "What passion(s) has God created within me?" As a Life Coach, I (Doug) have often asked clients what makes them cry or what makes them angry. The answers to these probing questions reveal issues and causes they feel deeply and reveal the Creator's unique fingerprint on their life. If you want to avoid wasting years, then take the time to discover the answers to these questions and then intentionally collaborate with God.

You have to be who you are. There is a sense in which you are the gift—you don't just have gifts. The mix of characteristics and experiences in your life make you who you are. Some people take this fact and drive it too far. When someone points out a negative characteristic in them they say, "That's just the way I am." That is painting with a pretty broad brush. There definitely are things about you that you cannot change. And there are many other things about you—many more than you might imagine—that you could change if you chose to do so.

If you really value something you can learn more about it. If you really believe something is important you can find a way to invest your 10,000 hours at it. If something really matters to you, you can keep scouring the world until you find partners who will lock arms with you to get it done.

If you love broad invigorating concepts but find details difficult to manage you must do two things. You must accept responsibility for details regardless of your skills. It just will be harder for you than for some. But secondly you must find a partner who is better with the details than you are.

If you are good with details but find it hard to see the big picture you must do two things. You don't necessarily have to draw the big picture but you must be willing to adopt one to look at. Secondly, you need to fall in behind someone with vision and help them pick up the pieces.

If you are future oriented you still have to take care of things today. If you are better at just doing the next thing you still have to lift up your eyes and look to the future.

If you're not so smart you had better link up with someone smarter than yourself. If you are not very creative you'd better become resourceful and draw on the creativity of others.

Do you see how the list goes on? Yes, you should work at discovering what makes you unique. And at the same time as you concentrate on your strengths, you must find ways to cover for your own weaknesses.

You will run into your share of critics along the zipline. Integrate their criticism into your perspective on yourself but don't let it define you. Now if the criticism points to a moral failure or character flaw, fix it. Bear in mind that critics are very quick to assume that any problem they see has its roots in character breakdown. That is not necessarily so. Take whatever someone tells you as their perspective on you. They are telling you what they see. They could be right or wrong but their reflection on your life must be worth something to you. You do want to get better at living, don't you? Then don't simply waste their input by ignoring it. Just work at it!

Find the combination of factors that gets you fired up in a positive, productive direction. Get passionate about something other than the distraction of the next big trend. Don't bother lining up at midnight to be the first one to get the new toy or watch the latest entertainment. All that will pass. In a few months everyone will wonder what the fuss was. When you tell your story after the fact it will sound silly.

The options for your personal engagement in something worthwhile cover a wide expanse. Explore your options and uncover the one thing that springs up like a geyser from your soul. Then find a way to do what you can to take that passion and turn it into something real that will last for eternity.

What do I get really animated about that has long-term family, societal and even eternal value? What must I set aside to invest more of me into that?

> *"I prefer to be a dreamer among the humblest,*
> *with visions to be realized,*
> *than lord among those without dreams and desires." Kahlil Gibran*

23
Encountering the Dream

Vision is seeing your preferred future. It is seeing something before it happens. It is anticipating a new adventure. It is vision that takes you there even though you might be fearful, nervous and wondering, "What have I got myself into?" as you step off from where it is safe to go where you have never gone before.

In their book *The Leadership Challenge*, Kouzes and Posner have researched the importance of vision, the ability to look ahead as one of the most sought after leadership traits. Vision gives clarity, purpose and direction. The message is clear, "Leaders must know where they're going if they expect others to willingly join them on the journey." In their study senior managers ranked "a leadership style of honesty and integrity" first and a "long-term vision and direction for the company" second. Vision is essential at a corporate level and even more so at the personal level.

When people understand their personal vision or purpose for life it assists them in determining the best path for the journey. Ziplining takes you stepping off the safe place of the platform and travelling to the next platform. It takes trusting the line, the harness, the clips and those who are coaching you to take the risk of the journey. If your personal vision is clear you will have a clear mental picture of your personal mission accomplished in the preferred future. Andy Stanley, in his book *Visioneering*, states that "Vision is a clear mental picture of what could be, fueled by the conviction that it should be." Conviction we believe for our vision is fueled by our personal calling to make a difference in this world using our talents, gifts and energy to impact others.

According to the Bible without vision people perish, drift or stumble towards the future. (Proverbs 29:18) They cast off restraint and become deadlocked by tradition, circumstances or attitudes that keep them from realizing their full potential as human beings created in the image of God. A clear personal vision is a powerful determinant for ending up somewhere on purpose with passion. Vision pulls you forward.

Do you have a powerful vision for your life? Every person needs to have their own unique statement, envisioning how they will fulfil God's purpose for their life.

Your vision needs to be written down. Here are some ideas for writing your personal vision statement of where you want to be in five years.

1. Determine your life purpose or mission.
2. Select the most definitive terms possible that relate strongly to you.
3. Make it concise with passionate wording.
4. Make it memorable by creating a personal picture or metaphor of your purpose.
5. Keep working it and persevere through the exercise to make it courageous.

A personal vision does not always require immediate action. Personal vision statements require patience and taking inventory of ourselves to move into our preferred future. Take time to investigate. Do a situational analysis of your life. Run it by others. Allow it to mature with time.

God grows us into the vision. What are the things you need to learn to be coached or mentored in so that this vision can be realized in your life? See it as an adventure that gets unpacked as God works providentially behind the scenes. He will orchestrate circumstances to provide what you need to step out into this new adventure. This process will stretch you and take you out of the comfort zone to the faith zone propelling you to your next destination.

Vision is also about timing—God's timing, your timing, circumstances lining up with preparation and planning. Taking a zipline requires planning, timing and preparation for a great exciting ride where you take in everything you experience. Learn from the journey and arrive at the end of the ride with experiences and new tools to take you to the next platform in your journey.

Is vision important for your journey? You bet it is. Without it life will come at you causing you to be reactionary. A clear vision causes you to respond and be proactive in life, causing you to make wise decisions that will take you to new places you have never gone before. With God's help you can be like the people of God in Joshua's time who followed God's plan for their life. They knew which way to go even though they had never been this way before. (Joshua 3:4) They had a clear vision of the promised land; they prepared, struggled and took courageous next steps. Their vision was clear and as a result conquered their fears, enemies and wanderings in the desert to experience the land "full of milk and honey." Without this vision they would have perished.

A clear vision for your life will evolve if you lay the need before the Lord every day. Ponder and respond to the thoughtful feedback of godly people in your life. Make the changes you know you must make while you wait for the vision to take shape.

Do I have a powerful vision for my life? Can I articulate it clearly and concisely? Am I living in such a way that the vision is not only possible but will probably become reality?

24
Adjusting the Dream

Your vision for life will energize you. You will have more spring in your step on the days when you feel like you are running in mud. Every day will bring the unexpected if you let it. This metaphor of ziplining brings exhilaration and fulfillment. If you get it right it also will bring you friends. You may not realize the impact you are making while riding the line. But be sure others will take note and either have some desire to follow or at least respect your example. If you stay on the platform saying, "We will see what happens to the next guy." they will also take note and exclaim, "That's no way to live when the zipline is right there in front of you."

Your vision for life will develop and grow if you let it. Sadly, most people start with vision and then with every setback dumb it down a notch. The older they get, the less they do, the less they try to do. Life is thinking, feeling and acting. Ziplining is acting. Action is what gets you the best bang for your buck. Right action brings you more positive feelings and more productive thoughts.

If you stop doing things because you were hurt last time you tried, your life will get slower and more and more depressing. You will get fatter and uglier. If your vision for life is to get fatter, uglier and more bored then you just do that. However, if you want the opposite you just have to go for it. Even if you don't get "it" the mere reaching forward will keep you supple and interesting. Yes, your body will start to slow down when you are over the hill but people will enjoy you more and you will enjoy them more as well.

Your vision for life will shift. Behind every experience stands some knowledge you didn't possess. Around every corner is another giant to slay and the new one is always a little different than the dead one in your path. Therefore, you need to always be a little light on your feet. You may think you will get something by stepping out and then get something entirely different. Make use of that experience you didn't expect. Don't sit down and suck your thumb for too long. Get up. Get going in a different direction as necessary. If you can't solve the problem look at it in a different way or enlarge the problem because every problem is actually a part of a bigger problem. Get bigger and you will get better. There will be times when it isn't working and you just have to quit on a path. Don't do that too soon. Make sure you get the full value out of every good event and every painful event.

Your vision for life will get stymied. All you can know about your future is that it won't be like the past and it won't be what you expect or hope for. It will be different. The younger you are the whiter the picket fence will be around the dream you call life. It won't end up that white. Guaranteed. And it won't be straight either. Life will end up as only a rough approximation of your original ideals at best. There are things you may build into your vision that will never come true. People will block your way. You will let yourself down. You will sin. You will get discouraged. You will hit a bad economy. You will fail. Your relationships won't be perfect. The sequence you imagine will get all garbled up. You will deal with detours. Make up your mind right now that you will not stop at the next roadblock and become a victim. The government, the boss, the economy, the industry and even the head hunter are not the only factors in why you didn't get to be the Prime Minister. You can't control the other guys. You must control yourself.

Your vision for life will never be realized if others don't take the ride with you. In particular, if you are married your spouse has to ride with you. You may agree to division of responsibility that allows you less or more adventure in separate parts of your lives but you must ride it together. If you think divorce is a happy option, why is it you can't find anyone who has experienced a divorce who highly recommends it? Many make the best of it after a divorce. Nobody who has been there recommends you start out with an experimental attitude and flippantly say, "Oh well, if it doesn't work out we can always split up." And if you can find somebody who suggests that is a good way to start, just get out your calculator and do a survey from all those who have tried that route. You will quickly find out that behind the face of it those who have gone through a messy divorce will tell you to bust everything out of your life that drives you in that direction. And by the way, messy as an adjective for divorce is only useful to amplify the term to the listener rather like saying "great big mess." Every great mess is also a big mess. In between the letters of the word divorce are buried those words "great big mess." So if you need to come to grips with the idea that your spouse isn't on the same track as you then for goodness sake and for your own good sake get off your line. Find a compromise or different direction you can both live with.

You can't make it alone. Make the personal adjustments you can and leave the results in the hands of your Creator.

When my dream gets blocked how do I respond?
Can I find a better way to move into the future
even when it isn't what I hoped for?

F. The Options

A. The Analogy   What a zipline has to do with life.

B. The Fear   Exploring the pressures to avoid the jump.

C. The Changes   Adopting a readiness for something new.

D. The Start   Finding the place and the team.

E. The Dream   Visioning a specific life direction.

F. The Options   Surveying all the possibilities.

G. The Lull   Recognizing a slow down.

H. The Stall   Handling the breakdowns.

I. The Thrill   Experiencing the exhilaration.

J. The Ride   Taking it as it comes.

K. The Awe   Watching God in action.

"Any customer can have a car painted any color that he wants so long as it is black." Henry Ford of the Model T

25

Defining Options

This is a world full of options. It used to be you could go to the store for milk and have three choices in two or three sizes. It was whole, 2% or skim. And the size was easy to choose. Now, there are over thirty choices. Go ahead count them. They have made an art form out of developing milk and milk substitutes. I can't imagine the cows would be happy if they knew.

When there appears to be too many options it is easy to dwell on your options and take far too long to make a choice. If you think it is hard to choose milk, try choosing the right toothpaste!

The key thing to do when identifying your main options for life is to find the realistic number of options to consider. For example, if you are choosing an educational institution, you can't look at them all or you will go insane. But you can quickly find three to five that meet your educational intentions. Stick with the smaller analysis of options until you find a compelling reason to add another. It just gets too complicated, especially if you are at a low ebb in life.

On the other hand, make sure you consider more than two options whatever the area of life you are looking at. For example, you probably can't view all the houses for sale in your price range in a big city. You have to narrow your search. But you don't want to simply buy the first house you see if you haven't done all the research. You know you won't find the perfect house but you have to find one you can live in. And yes, you can get carried away and overspend if you aren't careful. Many have made that mistake and found themselves house poor. Nice house. But you can't eat the extra 2 X 4s.

Let's back up a little. If you are in a slump and just feeling that life has become dull don't be too sure that you are considering the right area of life to change until you have thought it through. When boredom and disquiet arise you will tend to take it out on people. It is probably not the people around you that are making you grouchy. You just think it is.

So when you are looking for options don't assume that the boss is the problem or the husband or the kids or even the dog. You kick the dog. Then the dog bites the kid. Then the kid comes crying to you. Just saying, "I am sick of all this!" describes how you feel but it doesn't move you towards a solution.

If you are in a job you don't like and it really is the job, then do something. Start by doing a better job at the job you don't like while you are there and then leave the problems at the workplace. Don't go home and stew or gripe. Just let it go for now. You have to control the way you think. Learn that discipline. That isn't advice to stick your head in a chimney. It is advice to learn to control the things you can control. That will help you gain perspective.

Think on pen and paper. Well, that is old school. Think on your new tablet if you like. But by all means make sure you externalize for yourself. Just write. Writing helps you out of cyclical thinking. Most people in a funk just keep replaying the same thoughts. When you are writing you are too lazy to describe the same thing over and over. This forces you in the direction of thinking in a straight line.

When you think in a circle this is what you do. You ask yourself a question such as, "Why am I so depressed?" Then you supply the answer for yourself by saying, "I am depressed because nothing is working for me right now." Then you ask, "Why isn't anything working for me right now?" And you get back to, "I don't feel like trying any more and that makes me depressed." Can you guess where that leads? "Why am I so depressed?" You just did another loop around the same track. But you don't realize it unless you write it out. Further, if you write it out you can go back over your words and draw out the common themes. Depressed. Nothing working. Not trying. Do those themes sound like planning tools to you? Didn't think so.

Since you want a solution this is what to do. Go to www.lifeonthezipline.com/plan and register for an online planning tool to help you. It is free (for a limited time) so go and do it now. All the explanation you need is there for you. You will have your own private account and nobody will see what you write. (You can give your Life Coach access to your thinking if you choose to do so.) This online planning tool will help you find the area you need to work on. It will give you the place to express all your options so you don't forget. It will encourage you to keep track of all the factors that go into evaluating your options in a way that will give you a numerical score. It is really nifty! If you need a new zipline to ride don't miss this help at finding your best option.

What is my plan to start writing down my thoughts so I can get out of the recycling loop and come up with some options I haven't discovered yet?

> *"When you have two alternatives,*
> *the first thing you have to do is to look for the third*
> *that you didn't think about, that doesn't exist." Shimon Peres*

26
Discerning Alternatives

Hegel was a really smart guy who came up with a theory now called the "Hegelian dialectic." Never mind the history lesson. Here is a simplified explanation. Hegel said the first stage was Thesis (A). Then someone comes up with the next stage of Antithesis (B). Finally, balance is achieved by reaching Synthesis (C).

Here is how that might work in your life.

A. Thesis = My life is stalled. I don't like my body, my mind, my spirit, my spouse, my family, my friends, my career, my job, my house, my car, my country etc. (All of the above. Some of the above. Or other than the above.) Life sucks. I am not happy. All I want is to get permanently happy.

B. Antithesis = I have contrived a really fascinating alternative. If I could change my world and start again I think I could find permanent happiness or a reasonable facsimile. If you are in stage A you are stalled. And yes, you must do something or settle for a mediocre rest-of-my-life. But you wouldn't be this far into a book that promises "from Fear to Awe" in its sub-title if staying where you are was really acceptable to you. So what should you do? Perhaps you were hoping that "Zipline" in the title was going to show you how to get a really good stage B. Well, no.

B is never where it is at. Now Hegel may have said something about the necessity of B to pull the pendulum away from A. B is only necessary to help you gain a broader perspective. Let's say B is a revolution. A revolution can pull you away from A. And sometimes in history things smoulder until there is an explosion over A and then there is the complete chaos and damage of a revolution we are calling B. You want to find a sustainable option, not a temporary revolution.

If you don't make changes in you, not much will change for you. You will take you with you wherever you go. If you escape to some desert island where there are no tyrants you will take a nagging tyranny with you. Your own false expectations and hopes are the ultimate tyranny. You will find it too hot to lay naked on the lonely beach in the scorching sun. And besides the perfect friend you take with you would rather lie on an air mattress sipping a cold drink in the pool. So you will still be thwarted. B thinking is just like A. Life sucks there too. You just don't know how similar B can be to A yet.

You want C.

Remember A and B?

A. Thesis = My life is stalled.

B. Anti-thesis = I have contrived a really fascinating alternative. My alternative eliminates all the problems of A.

C. Synthesis = I found the adjustments I needed to make in me so that I didn't just jump into B. I thought it through. I changed. And the change in me heightened my ability to see life more properly. Then I was able to go out and make some adjustments for me.

C brings together the best worlds possible. Your striving for an ideal in B can be put to use in making the adjustments you alone can make to A to create C. It would be nice if you had some help. But you must take responsibility to realistically evaluate A. You want to mix in some of the elements and ideals of B so that you can find C to live in without causing wasteful and debilitating collateral damage for yourself and the others around you.

If you have hit the wall in some way you are in a dangerous place. You are in danger of exploding from A into B without making sound judgments. Don't let the despair of your life-stall cause you to over-react. But on the other hand don't just accept failure as your destiny. If you simply implement a small percentage of what you are reading here, you will find that stoppage of your life to be a temporary condition. It will get better when you make the right choices.

That evolution may take many months or years before your chance comes. Just wait for it productively by changing the things you should change along the way. In extreme cases, your life could end and like Martin Luther King you may never attain your "promised land." But who would argue that his life didn't contribute to a better world for many? He was significant. You too can be significant. Your significance will be dotted along the trail you left behind that you may have long since forgotten. If you live every day to its fullest even when you feel like you are beating on a hard wall, you may not make much of a mark on that wall. However, you will leave an impact in which others will find hope.

> *"...we also glory in our sufferings, because we know that suffering produces perseverance; perseverance, character; and character, hope. And hope does not put us to shame, because God's love has been poured out into our hearts through the Holy Spirit, who has been given to us." (Romans 5:3-5)*

What skills and character traits do I need to develop so I can always find the best solution?

> *"By three methods we may learn wisdom: First, by reflection, which is noblest; Second, by imitation, which is easiest; and third by experience, which is the bitterest." Confucius*

27
Determining the Right Change

Young people often have big plans for their lives. Older people often do what they can to convince the young people that what they want to achieve is not possible. Perhaps they forget they were once young with wild-eyed dreams. But it is more likely that they want to preserve the next generation from the bruises and bumps they are about to face.

The job of the Life Coach is to help all clients form their lofty ideals into practical plans. Nothing is as easy as it looks. Young people need to put intensity into their efforts to achieve what their forbearers failed to achieve. It takes care to match idealism with realism and at the same time not squelch enthusiasm.

Defining the correct choices to make in life takes much more than a strong feeling. It takes the due diligence of research, interviews with wise counsellors, in depth study of the Word of God and circumstantial opportunity. The goal of all this work is to get to a resounding "yes!" One should never dampen down the enthusiasm to keep people in a narrow and safe range. The narrow and safe range is usually boring, grey and sad.

None of us want to live in grey sadness. However, that's exactly what happens when we refuse to let God move us and use us in different ways. A grey coloured life is a symptom revealing that a change is needed. The Little River Band captured the longing of those stuck in the predictable life. They sang,

> "Time for a cool change.
> I know that it's time for a cool change.
> Now that my life is so prearranged
> I know that it's time for a cool change."

While T.S. Eliot warned that the greatest sin was to do the right thing for the wrong reason, you should also be warned that it is possible to do the wrong thing for the right reason. Like a boomerang, making change for change's sake may bring you right back to the grey and sadness again. You may need a change, but it must be the right change.

It depends on the impact of the area in which you must make a choice. Big decisions have high impact; smaller decisions have less impact. The impact of the decision will determine how much thought you need to make. But you need to remember that seemingly small choices that take you even one small increment off course when amplified over time can land you in that dark forest. Constantly monitor your thinking to make sure you are living out your vision and values.

The first step is to look at all the reasonable options and predict the probability of each one taking you closer to the vision for your life that you worked out. So, let's create an example. Suppose you are thinking you are headed to a dead end in your job. You may immediately think about getting your resumé out there and testing the job market. That is good. You do want to find out if there are any interesting opportunities. But you do have other options. You could look into part-time additional education to extend your abilities in the same field you are in. Or you could think of a complete career change. You certainly can start by doing a check up from the neck up to assure that you are working at your optimum right where you are. You are an ambassador right there regardless of whether the boss or the company knows it.

Next you should isolate the factors that come into play for each viable option. Fantasy options don't count. You have to work with what you have in front of you, following the job theme. If you move to another town how will that impact all the individuals in your family—positively and negatively? Will this take them closer to the plan of God for their individual lives as far as you can tell? Plan to list every possible factor you can think of on both sides of the option. Once you list all the factors assign a weight to them based on how important they are to you. Once you have exhausted your thinking add up your score on each option. This won't take months but take a few days or weeks to sort it all out.

Keep everyone who is impacted by your decision informed. Don't cheat any stakeholders by springing something on them.

Make every effort to keep yourself from playing mental tricks to get what you are lusting for instead of doing what is right.

There is a lot more help for you on this subject at www.lifeonthezipline.com/plan. Sign up for a free account and follow through. You will be glad you took the time to make a quality decision based on all the considerations available.

What mechanisms have I put in place in my life to keep myself from making foolish choices? Am I willing to think and plan out my next big decision? How will I demonstrate that I am striving to do the will of God?

28
Knowing When It's Time

Finding just the right time to jump seems like tricky business. More often than not you will identify that it was the correct time after you actually put your decision into action. But that doesn't make it any easier looking forward.

You have found the right time to jump after you have done all your research and you have confidence that you can't say "no" to the jump. It is possible to go on researching for the rest of your life and still not gather complete information. To say that you have done all your research is to say that you have done all the research you know you should do.

The right time to jump comes when you have no other option. By the process of elimination you can remove many potential options because when you analyze the factors the weight of evidence points in a clear direction. Some potential options for you have a deal breaker built in. The deal breaker is a factor that you will not violate no matter what. Sometimes the deal breakers are based on your underlying moral values. For example, you may have heard that facetious statement, "Murder maybe; divorce never!" That points to a moral conviction on two counts. Obviously, to the person making this statement they are really saying divorce is no more an option than murder. That doesn't mean that divorce might not hit from the other side.

When it comes to sin some people say, "I would never commit adultery." But you don't actually know what you might do if a compelling and seducing option presents itself at the moment of great vulnerability.

> *"So, if you think you are standing firm, be careful that you don't fall!"*
> *(1 Corinthians 10:12)*

There are more deal breakers. For example, you could have a financial commitment that you fail to complete on time. It isn't necessarily moral, but you might refuse to take a compelling job because the salary is too low. You might not be willing to move away from a particular geographical location because it would take you away from your extended family. The list is highly individualized; but if you have settled exactly where the fences are you will not jump, you can cross a lot of potential options off your list.

You have found a good option for life if it is consistent with your well thought out life vision. You merely have to ask yourself if this moves you closer to fulfilling your life calling. Sometimes you have to take long detours for that calling. You won't always be presented with a perfect option; therefore you need to expect some ambiguity. There will be times when your life calling doesn't come with a paycheck. You will have to do other things to supply the money for life so you can do what you have to do in other hours. Life callings don't come in neat 40 hour per week packages. If you are married spousal support is essential. Support is not acquiescence due to the expectation your spouse has that you will keep nagging like a spoiled child until you get your way. Spousal support doesn't necessarily mean spousal involvement. It does, however, mean that your spouse will not resent your new commitment. It might mean that there are some distasteful elements to your new zipline but you both are prepared for those together.

If you have children living in a home with you, you must consider the impact any decision you make has on them. Involve them in the discussion of the pros and cons of any particular option and ask them to enhance the discussion. Respect them in every way. Acknowledge their feelings. If, for example, you are considering moving across the country and they raise the issue about losing their friends, don't just tell them they will make new friends. They already knew that. Commiserate with them about how hard it is to lose friends. Tell them stories about friends that you lost. Explain that shifting relationships is something that will happen with them over and over again in life. Invite them to tell you how they feel and empathize with their feelings. You can come back the next day with your discussion about making new friends. Also bear in mind that you have life shaping teachable moments when you are facing big choices. You teach the others around you how to process decision-making events in their own lives.

Of course not all decisions you must make are life shaking major moves. But if you get good at the big decisions you will handle the lesser decisions nicely. If you are not sure about what to do, delay your jump until you have complete information or have exhausted all the current opportunities. That being said, most people when they look back recognize that they should have made a decision sooner. If there is no more information to gather and there is nothing else you can do because your environment has closed in on you then just jump. It is best to not wait until the pain and fear of where you are supersedes the pain of the uncertainty about the jump you know you must make. Don't let stubborn tenacity about what could happen make things worse if your idea isn't going to happen.

Sooner is usually better than later for most people because most of us hesitate too long. Take the earliest wise choice and you will be glad you did sooner than later.

Will waiting any longer bring in more information about this decision?
Exactly what steps do I need to take
to complete my research and arrive at peace?

G. The Lull

A.	The Analogy	What a zipline has to do with life.
B.	The Fear	Exploring the pressures to avoid the jump.
C.	The Changes	Adopting a readiness for something new.
D.	The Start	Finding the place and the team.
E.	The Dream	Visioning a specific life direction.
F.	The Options	Surveying all the possibilities.
G.	**The Lull**	**Recognizing a slow down.**
H.	The Stall	Handling the breakdowns.
I.	The Thrill	Experiencing the exhilaration.
J.	The Ride	Taking it as it comes.
K.	The Awe	Watching God in action.

29
Avoiding Grey

The Beatles imagined a life of ease—every one of us having all we need. They sang,

"Sky of blue and sea green in our yellow submarine.
We all live in yellow submarine."

That's not true, is it? It's a lie. There are numbers of things that trap people in grey tubes not pretty yellow ones.

A brush that colours our lives grey may involve our closest relationships. During a season of our life we may enter into a relationship that is quite unhealthy. The Bible warns of being "unequally yoked." That word picture was really clear until we all moved to the city. Any farmer knows he is in trouble if he has two mismatched animals trying to pull his farm instrument. The imbalance makes it really tough if not impossible.

With people the obvious application is in the choice of a life partner. The time to sort this out is before marriage. If your potential partner does not share your faith and values, then make the jump—get out now. If that person verbally deflates you or physically intimidates you, make the jump. If they are only interested in receiving love and affirmation, but not expressing it back, make the jump. But this could also be applied to business partnerships and other relationships. Study the concept carefully. (2 Corinthians 6:14-7:1)

Too many people work in a place and at a task that sucks the life out of them. There are creative people who work on a factory line, relational people who work in isolation and introverts who do social work. Those are just a few samples of proverbial square pegs in round holes. This same principle applies to communities of worship. Some worship God in a traditional setting, but they possess a demonstrative personality. Others may be surrounded by those expressive free-style worshippers, but personally need the richness of seasoned prayers and liturgy. Finding the appropriate environment and method for self-expression is a key to stay out of the grey submarine. You need a good fit. Define it. Search for it. Find it. Then jump.

A younger man came to me (Doug) one time and sat in my office. I had the privilege of mentoring this gifted person for six years. He said to me, "I am frustrated. When I first began working with you, I felt you had much to teach me. I was like a sponge. But lately, I feel that I am not learning anything new from you." I appreciated his candor. He was experiencing arrested development. He had grown as much as he could in the present situation. It was time for a change. He needed to grow. I completely understood. After all, I am not an unlimited well of knowledge. He needed to work with someone else with different gifts who could challenge him in new ways. Or perhaps he was ready to spread his wings on his own and become a mentor himself. I assured him that I would do whatever I could to help him jump.

Yes, there are also many other circumstances in people's lives where change is required and a jump is absolutely necessary to leave the grey behind. Each of us can lie to God, lie to others and even ourselves. We project that everything is okay. However, our body will eventually tell us the truth. When we are consistently stressed, fatigued, exhausted, and ill with headaches and a variety of depressive ailments, a jump is necessary. Are you tired of the grey? Are you ready to say "no" to more wasted years? In the classic *Moby Dick*, Melville writes,

> "The chick that's in him pecks the shell. Twill soon be out."

Jesus asked Peter an interesting question. Peter had been fishing and was evidently attached to his tools and nets.

> *"'Simon son of John, do you truly love me more than these?' Peter answered, 'Yes, Lord, you know that I love you.'" (John 21:16)*

Jesus was in no way convinced that Peter was being honest and forced the question further. Peter is not the only one who struggles with honesty on this matter. Within each of us is what Blaise Pascal terms "The God-shaped vacuum." But instead of reducing our needs and filling this void with God, we pack our lives with more stuff. Robin Sharma, in *The Monk Who Sold His Ferrari*, wrote,

> "If you always want more than you have how can you be happy?"

Yet, in spite of the emptiness, we purchase and gather more pretending each purchase will be enough. Insert your own name if you dare. "_____, do you truly love me more than these?" On this matter of materialism, you need to simplify. Jim Elliot, a young missionary who lost his life in the Amazon at age 28 once said, "He is no fool who gives what he cannot keep to gain what he cannot lose."

He had it figured out. And he lived it out until he died. He jumped; he died young but having lived a full life.

You want and need a full life. You need to make the jump.

Do I know what's stopping me? How will I find out what is stopping me and how to eliminate the power of that factor? Who will help me?

30
Admitting Trouble

Grey was the colour of my life. I (Doug) dreamed that I was in a submarine. The walls, doors, and ladders were all steel grey. I was in a corridor feeling depressed. As I moved down the hall and opened a door to the left I entered a room full of colour. It was a church sanctuary filled with people who were physically present, but emotionally absent. In spite of the few on the platform leading in lively praise music, those in the audience were at best apathetic. John the Revelator's words about a people reputed as being alive, but really dead seemed fitting. Compelled to do something, I stepped onto the platform and encouraged the people to repeat a mantra, "Love, joy, peace, love, joy, peace, love, joy…." Suddenly the atmosphere was charged with energy. My job was done. Having passed the microphone back to the worship leader, I exited the room and closed the door. Then leaning back against the grey steel wall, I sighed with exasperation, "What was that all about?"

There was movement. Although the submarine had been floating at the surface, it was going down. Quickly, I pulled myself together and went back down the corridor to where I had been standing previously. I opened the hatch and stepped onto the edge. Before me were one hundred and fifty foot waves as those imagined in Sebastian Junger's, *Perfect Storm*. I contemplated, "No one could survive thirty seconds out there." Nevertheless, another second surrounded by the grey and the façade of colour in that sanctuary was more than I could bear. I jumped! Immediately I awoke from the dream. Rather than feeling dread at the prospect of drowning, I was filled with exhilaration.

William Young wrote,

> "Dreams are sometimes important you know. They can be a way of opening up the window and letting the bad air out."

The Bible is filled with accounts of God speaking to men and women during their sleep. Abram, Joseph, Daniel, and Peter are just a few. Is it because they were too dense to listen to His voice with their conscious mind that God resorted to their subconscious? I don't know. I do know that when God is prompting us to do something that requires a good measure of courage, He finds creative ways to lead and affirm us. Like Daniel, I recorded my dream in a journal.

I wondered if God was leading me to a place where I would be required to disembark from all that was familiar. The great ones had to do it. Abram was required to pull up his tent pegs and relocate in the direction of the unknown. Peter was compelled to let go of the boat in order to walk on water. Jesus too! He was in glory and then let go to become one of us. He emptied Himself and was made in human likeness. Each one of us will come to a place and realize we should not stay where we are. This moment has sometimes been referred to as the Second Call or the Second Journey. It is always framed by the question, "What am I supposed to do with the rest of my life?"

Lest you wonder, my story reaches a high measure of resolve and we will get to that later in the book.

But for now, understand that there often comes a time when life altering decisions must be made. And the prelude to a better path is often uncomfortable to say the least. When a person finds themselves in this "dark forest" or the "steel grey corridor of a submarine" they often suppose their position to be unusual, untenable and even terminal. Unfortunately, some, seeing no way out, take the ultimate way out and take their own lives. More people than you might imagine have seriously contemplated that solution, which only looks like a solution at the time.

It is faint comfort but comfort nonetheless to realize that there is a positive way out as yet to be discovered. In His mercy God always delays and/or diminishes the horrible judgment we all deserve. In His grace God always provides a way. Always. Not always imminent or obvious but always. If you are in doubt, memorize this and cling to it.

"No temptation has overtaken you except what is common to mankind. And God is faithful; he will not let you be tempted beyond what you can bear. But when you are tempted, he will also provide a way out so that you can endure it." (1 Corinthians 10:13)

Am I brave enough to admit it
when my inner self is trying to get my attention?
What evidence do I give to show I face "grey submarines" with courage?

> *"Life is like a coin. You can spend it any way you want.*
> *But you can only spend it once." Lillian Dickson*

31
Wasting Time

Wasting time—those words reflect on common human experience. You have the option to wallow in the thoughts and emotions generated by the wasted years in the grey submarine. Or you can figure out something to do next. Van Morrison wrote a song entitled *Wasted Years*. Here are some of the lyrics.

"Wasted years been brainwashed by lies
Oh yes I have
Oh wasted years
I'm talking about wasted years
Oh I'm not seeing eye-to-eye
I just can't see the things I should see
Wasted years, baby
I was taking the wrong advice
I know you was, I know you was
And I was too
All alone I'm travelling
Travelling through these wasted years."

Invest far more time anticipating the days ahead than you do analyzing the years left behind. The place in which you find yourself need not be your permanent dwelling. You can't control everything about your present or your future but you can make the best of every situation.

If you let the safety of the sameness of your present situation rule when you should take a risk and do something else, some day you will look back on more wasted years. It gets really complicated if your family doesn't see your greyness and is quite content to stay put. That makes it hard to change locations and it certainly makes it hard for you to move to a new career. You will do well to bring them along with your big change idea. Remember, these thoughts of your big jump didn't rise in you in a day and you will have to give those you love some time to adjust to the idea.

What if they never get on board with you? Then you have to work out a compromise of some sort. You will need to find some creative diversion. But, for crying out loud, don't waste endless hours on the Internet in the middle of the night. Nothing good happens on the Internet when you are supposed to be getting the rest you need.

When the other circumstances simply don't line up for you to ride the zipline of your dreams perhaps you have to build your own. That is far harder than riding a pre-built system. But if the option you yearn for doesn't exist then go out and create it. At least, at first entertain the option by studying the subject. If you haven't read at least a thousand pages on the subject that is bugging you, you just need to try harder.

Some people say, "I don't read." To which I say, "Did you not go to school and learn how?" What you mean is something different. You read alright. You just don't like it for some reason. Lazy people don't read. They don't read because they are lazy, not because they don't read. Discipline yourself to take in the information you need. You got this far in this book and that is good evidence that you do so read. How much pain has this been so far? What really did you miss by putting in a few hours here?

There are many other things to do while you are waiting. Take on a new personal challenge. Get a new exercise regime. Get your nutritional needs in better shape. Study the science of sleep. Start a productive hobby. Help somebody. You have far more control over yourself than you think.

Do the very best you can. Become a better person in every way possible and you will find that those you love will warm up to your big idea. If not, your big idea might just fade away. Try to find an even bigger plan you can all agree with. Maybe the zipline you are dreaming about is just child's play compared to the jungle canopy ride God has for you!

Are the people around me respecting me more and more every day? What
changes do I have the opportunity to make while my life is on hold?

32
Valuing the Dark Days

Many have written their story of dark days in prison, poverty, disease or despair. As you read such dark stories you wonder how they could ever survive. The authors often marvel at the same thing. But there is something about being alive that gives a person a sense of vitality no matter how faint. Perhaps you have had the privilege of being at the side of a friend or loved one in their fleeting final moments. There is profound sadness but there is also a preciousness.

I (Gary) had the privilege of visiting a dying friend the same day our daughter Rebekah was married. Her friend, my friend's daughter, left a vacancy in the wedding party that day. There was an empty space because she needed to be at home with the family. My friend Gord was dying at home. I hadn't seen him for many months and visitors were not allowed. But we respectfully broke into those sacred moments. As I entered his bedroom and saw Gord's emaciated body, he awoke and glowed with a surprised "Gary!" whispering from his faltering lips. We gripped each other's hands and I promised him I would see him again in Glory. That was many years ago now. But the preciousness of that day lives on as I write with tears of fond memory in my eyes. The subsequent years have not been easy for the family but the good memories of great times in life still bounce around and bring comfort. We were tired after fully participating in the wedding and reception. Gord's home was over an hour away. We might have missed that final good-bye if we had given in to the exhaustion and not made that memorable visit. Gord died the next day.

Don't miss today while you wait for tomorrow. Don't strive against the leash looking for the next tree. There are plenty of things to sniff out right now! Appreciate what is right there under your nose. Tomorrow will come soon enough. Today is the best day you have left until you get another one. Make this the best of days.

If you know the provision of God in your life why on earth would you think that what He has done in the past He won't do for you again and again?

> *"Now listen, you who say, 'Today or tomorrow we will go to this or that city, spend a year there, carry on business and make money.' Why, you do not even know what will happen tomorrow. What is your life? You are a mist that appears for a little while and then vanishes. Instead, you ought to say, 'If it*

is the Lord's will, we will live and do this or that.' As it is, you boast in your arrogant schemes. All such boasting is evil. If anyone, then, knows the good they ought to do and doesn't do it, it is sin for them." (James 4:13-17)

That is a wake up buzzer. Is there much different today for you than there was for James' readers in the first century?

You can't get much more direct than that, can you? Do some good you know to do in this day and stop the sin!

The concept of a zipline may be a little shallow because it conjures up images of exhilarating recreation and breathless fun. Commercial zipline rides are a rather safe and predictable affair to be enjoyed for a few short minutes. But when we take the zipline as a metaphor for life and especially its defining decision moments the imagery gets far more serious.

There is a good deal of instruction in this book about overcoming adversity, difficulty and sin. These strategies and tactics are seldom expounded. But when you work as a Life Coach you realize how hard it is for people to get moving forward. And as we write this book together we recognize how much help people need with basic life skills. Our society and even our churches have drifted into denial about the risks of life. We would rather focus on the rewards. And the rewards of walking with Jesus are astounding and out of this world! But you have to learn to take the right jumps every day in order to experience that inner confidence and assurance.

The more dark days you experience and manage well, the more you will value this present day. When you live in day-tight compartments and appreciate each moment life is so much more fulfilling. This isn't a day you "have to" live. This is a day you "get to" live. And today may be the day you get to take out the garbage or it might be the day you get to visit a world premier of something. This day is so special; don't waste it!

What will I do within the next 24 hours that I have been putting off? Once I get that difficult piece completed, how will I feel? How will I reward myself for a job well done?

> *"Forgiveness is the power granted to each of us to release us from a lifetime of anger and bitterness." Grant D. Fairley*

33
Seeking Forgiveness

When I (Robin) was leading one organization one of the members of the board had caused me a lot of damage. I had a very thick file folder with all the emails, letters and articles he had sent to me and members of our organization criticizing my leadership. He finally resigned from the board and took about 70 members with him. The amazing thing is that three years later I was still carrying resentment for what this man did to me.

God convicted me that I was holding back the blessing. I needed to go to his home and ask forgiveness not expecting anything from him. After praying and clearly working out the wording I went to ask the man for forgiveness for the resentment I had against him. He was surprised since he said he wasn't the easiest guy to deal with at a board level. He did not apologize for any of the stuff he had done to me but then again I was there to deal with my sinful issues. I asked him to forgive me and he did. I left that day free and forgiven. The next few years I experienced some amazing blessings in my life and in the life of the organization I was leading. I simply acted upon God's prompting in my life. A great burden was lifted off my shoulders.

The Apostle Paul said a great example for us and exhorted us to follow in his steps.

> *"All of us, then, who are mature should take such a view of things. And if on some point you think differently, that too God will make clear to you. Only let us live up to what we have already attained." (Philippians 3:15-16)*

Notice that when you have a clear focus and simple mindedness to win the prize it is God's responsibility to make it clear to you when you are living otherwise. This is an important principle. When your conscience is clear you are able to move forward wholeheartedly. You cannot properly lead your own life or your family's let alone an organization if you do not have the confidence that comes from a totally clean heart.

You are definitely going to stall or stay stalled in your life if there is the guilt of unconfessed sin nagging you. This is a double edged sword. On the one hand, God will withdraw blessing from your life if you are not walking closely with Him. And on the other hand, you will not have the confidence in your personality that you need to ride the zipline with full engagement.

It is easy to divert attention from your own guilt by saying to yourself, "I was wrong but he/she was even more wrong than me; therefore, I am going to wait until he/she confesses his/her sin to me." You may wait a very long time. During that time the sin will continue to poison you. Even if the person does initiate reconciliation you will have wasted all that time. Days turn into weeks; weeks turn into years; years turn into decades. You will be no further ahead than you would have been if you had confessed your own sin within hours. Why waste so much life? Those days can never be recaptured. You will just sink deeper into that dark forest.

If you find that you can't look someone in the eye because of some statement or event you need to do something about it. If the issue pops into your mind repeatedly and it is keeping you from your life's work, take action.

Be careful and precise in the action you take. Always think carefully before you speak. You cannot unspeak and stuff the words back in your mouth. You must convey the correct attitude. Your objective is to demonstrate deep Christian maturity.

> *"... speaking the truth in love, we will grow to become in every respect the mature body of him who is the head, that is, Christ." (Philippians 4:13-15)*

As you plan what to say think in this framework, "I have come to understand how wrong I was in _____. I have come to ask you to forgive me." Don't add a "but." The other person's side of the problem isn't the issue. You made your own choices and need to accept responsibility for your own sins.

How you convey your message is more important than the words you use. When you talk to the person from whom you are asking forgiveness they might want to pick a fight and let you know how wrong you were. Bear this proverb in mind and live it out.

> *"A gentle answer turns away wrath, but a harsh word stirs up anger."*
> *(Proverbs 15:1)*

Never meet the other person's harsh words with your own. Nobody wins when you do that. At the same time, deal with the issue and don't avoid it. The best way to do this is to ask questions without accusing tones or built in assumed answers. Listen carefully and accurately. To make sure you understand repeat back to the speaker the message you have heard. Make sure you don't project onto the other person motives that aren't there. You can be assertive without raising your voice. Assertiveness is the ability to express yourself, your feelings, your needs and your wants.

Go ahead. Plan that meeting. You will free up your ride on that old zipline!

> ***Who have I wronged? What is my plan to achieve reconciliation?***
> ***When will I get this done and find freedom again?***

H. The Stall

A.	The Analogy	What a zipline has to do with life.
B.	The Fear	Exploring the pressures to avoid the jump.
C.	The Changes	Adopting a readiness for something new.
D.	The Start	Finding the place and the team.
E.	The Dream	Visioning a specific life direction.
F.	The Options	Surveying all the possibilities.
G.	The Lull	Recognizing a slow down.
H.	**The Stall**	**Handling the breakdowns.**
I.	The Thrill	Experiencing the exhilaration.
J.	The Ride	Taking it as it comes.
K.	The Awe	Watching God in action.

34
Grinding to a Halt

You have hit the wall. You have no energy left for the task. It all just simply seems like too much for you. You wonder where you went wrong. But you can't figure that out. It all feels like a trap.

That might not be your situation at this moment but perhaps there have been times in your life when you felt this way. Then again you might just feel an overwhelming sense of boredom with life. All the challenge may be gone. All the relationships seem distant or stale.

There will be times when you feel that your zipline has ground to a halt. The best comfort you can imagine is to get off the line and get to another. But then, that isn't usually possible without incredible cost. Sometimes they call it a "mid-life crisis" but while such desires to quit and start again may bunch together at mid-life, they can hit at any stage. The fantasies often find expression in temporary diversions or detours. There are many versions of it; you are somewhat familiar with it because you have seen others jump off and find a new zipline. The classic method is to start an affair with someone who seems to be a better choice than your mate. Everything in you finds that other person more attractive. You start to believe it. "He/she really understands me like no other." "I feel the affirmation I have longed for since I was a rejected child." "No really, it is not the sex; it is that I have finally found my soul mate." "He completes me." "She fills me up." The interesting thing is that you can believe this stuff as if you were the first person to ever experience it.

There is another common response when life grinds to a halt. You just accept the sameness. You might not like the place you find yourself but you do find it familiar. Familiarity has a perverse way of bringing comfort. Then the comfort may wear out and you end up with contempt for your life. As the expression goes, "Familiarity breeds contempt." or at least boredom. It is as if you are forced to watch the same bad movie over and over. You might know that this is a waste of your life but at the same time you aren't ready to make a change.

Do you recall chapter 26 where we introduced Hegel? Where you are is A. And it is really a dark place. What you are thinking is about B. When the pain of A is acute the pleasure of B overshadows the potential danger or cost. B looks and feels so attractive.

Don't jump! Too many people try stage B out and get in a mess. They leave situation A and go searching for the ideal alternative —B. The pain or negativity of A easily creates a false hope in B. Most people who dump A find out later that it wasn't as bad as they thought it was while they were living in it. In fact, it might have been as much as 80% good. But the 20% bad was all they could see at the time. Any escape from the mess of A looks attractive. You are in a mess. You may have created the mess. Perhaps you can save face by taking option B even though it isn't truly what you need. It just looks good and you may even be able to sell it to others as the wise alternative. But underneath it all there is more to the story.

How many people do you know who have jumped out of a marriage because the sex was bad? But that really important component of a marriage represents less than 1% of the time in the marriage. It is the thinking about it or the lack of it that can create an overbalance in your definition. You aren't getting enough so your fantasy makes up a new world where that is all you get.

That same emotionally charged thinking can get you to quit a job or even leave a country. Suppose that 10% of what the boss does irritates you like sand paper underwear. In this case you could get so irritated that you can't even think about the other 90% of the boss's behaviour. All you can do is reiterate in your soul the wounding comments or impossible expectations that come once in a while. You think you might murder the boss if you stay. You forget how much you enjoy the other people around you in the workplace. You forget how good you are at your job and how much you actually enjoy the challenge. You forget the pay at the end of the week. So you just quit the situation and look for your dream.

There are more alternatives than A and B. That is really important for you to grasp. All or nothing thinking is not the product of wisdom. The purpose of this book is to help you with some more information and to stimulate you to find that better way. You will have to do the hard work yourself. You will have to think into spaces of your mind you have left unexplored. You will need to talk with the right people to help you do that.

You must be willing to change. Here is a repeat sentence from earlier in the book. In order for things to change for you something must change in you.

What emotions have a way of running over my judgment
if I am not careful? Do I have clear conviction about what needs to change
and if so, what am I doing about it?

35

Fantasizing about the Future

The Dog Whisperer, Cesar Milan indicates that my (Doug's) dog has a problem. His mind is not in a balanced state. For example, when I take him for a walk, he is unable to enjoy the experience because his mind is focussed on any moving thing up ahead. He completely misses out on the sights and scents immediately around him. He bears down and pulls. His tongue hangs out. He heaves so hard; he chokes himself, but not enough to stop. When I force him to sit, his eyes dart every which way and his head swivels like an image from some horror movie. He is not unlike a lot of people who never pause long enough to absorb the beauty and wonder of the moment they are in. Busy fools!

Another way we miss the thrill of the adventure is always to be looking to the destination.

There have been groups who have so expected Christ's return that they gathered themselves to a certain location and waited. They forgot the parable of the ten minas, a lesson about using our gifts until the owner returns (Luke 19). Similarly, we must not be so focussed on where God is leading us that we miss the miracles on the way.

Michael Card sang,

"There is a joy in the journey
There's a light we can love on the way
There is a wonder and wildness to life
and freedom for those who obey."

A young man in his quest to become like his teacher asked how long it would take to become as wise. The grizzled old man answered, "Five years perhaps."
"That is too long" replied the understudy. "I will apply myself twice as much."
"Then it will take you even longer, perhaps ten years" answered the teacher.
"Then I must read and retain knowledge through study from early morning to late evening."
"It will take you at least fifteen years."
"Why is it you tell me it will take even longer when I determine to devote more attention to becoming wise like you?"

"Listen, young man. With one eye on the destination, you only have one eye left to guide you on the journey's path."

There is no doubt that the future draws you. The air of the future always seems fresher than the air you must breathe today. In many ways that highly oxygenated fresh air is what you need. And if you decide to make the best out of the available air you have today you might just get there some day. Today has incredible advantages. As you read this it is likely that you are sitting somewhere. Take a moment and look up. Do you see a colour or shape you like in the room? Is there a window to look out? Is there anything out there worth looking at for a moment? How about the position your body is in right now? Is there anything comfortable about that? How about the chair you are in? Perhaps you are wearing some favourite comfortable clothes? It is highly unlikely that you cannot find something you like about this precise moment. Even if you are on a commuter train standing holding to a stanchion with one hand and with this book in the other, the familiar motions sounds, smells and jostles give you a sense of being alive in this moment, do they not? That sheer sense of life is what you have at this moment. It is precious. Take it for what it is.

This is the only day you have. The future will come soon enough. Make up your mind to stop the day dreaming about how things could be and work at making yourself the person you will need to be should that dream ever show up in reality. The biggest component you must have for tomorrow is perspiration not inspiration. You can start to sweat it out today, no matter what the growth area.

It starts with the way you allow your mind to think. You do have the capacity to control how you think. You may not even know it. You may have developed such a habit to let your mind wander that you never capture your thoughts and redirect them.

> *"We demolish arguments and every pretension that sets itself up against the knowledge of God, and we take captive every thought to make it obedient to Christ." (2 Corinthians 10:5)*

Notice the aggressive powerful words in that one verse. This is war. "Demolish arguments." "Demolish every pretension." How many pretensions? "Take captive every thought." How many thoughts? This is not for cartoon characters and wimps. Real men and women don't allow their minds to wander away from the knowledge of God and obedience to Christ. Are you a real man or a real woman?

On a scale of 1 to 10 how much do I control my thinking and point it Godward? What will I start today to take that up a few notches?

36
Living in La La Land

La La Land is closer than you may think. It is the place where people go when fantasy gives the comfort their reality seldom affords. Your wishes for the future can take you deep into fantasy if you let them. I (Gary) had a neighbour once who loved the Harry Potter world. He said that he believed that somewhere in this world that sort of magical experience must be real. No kidding. He, an intelligent adult, was serious. He lived a very sad life because he invested almost all his time in fantasy and never got around to cutting his grass. Recently he died. The sadness is still with me.

You say, "Well I am not like that." Good. But are there elements of your thinking that point you in that direction? Here are some checkpoints for you to think about.

When people put in too much time relaxing they often are in La La Land. Everyone needs appropriate rest. Reading the occasional novel, playing a game, doing a puzzle or going to the odd sporting event is a big part of letting your brain recharge. When Albert Einstein was attempting to solve an overwhelming problem he often would clear his brain with music—he played the piano. He was no slouch. He had learned how to maximize his mental productivity. If you are so inactive, however, that your house is unpainted and the garbage is piled high you really need to rethink.

Killing time is murder. Time is the most precious commodity you have. You never know how much of it you are going to get but you can be precisely sure that it is doled out to you at exactly the same rate as it is to other people. Killing time won't make you feel like doing something useful; it will only reinforce the killing time habit. If you find yourself consistently giving in to the natural desire to do nothing then you will likely retreat into La La Land and occupy the precious moments of life with day dreaming.

How many people have you run into in life who have told you they would like to do something but they are too old, too poor, too busy or too you-pick-the-idea? Any excuse will do if you don't really want to pay the price to do something. You might, for example confess, "I would really like to go back to school and get another degree." Then you hasten to add, "But that would take me about 7-10 years part time. And I would be 10 years older when I finish." So the next question is, "How old will you be in 10 years if you don't do it?" Time is constant. What you choose to do with it is variable and creates the illusion of elasticity. At least be honest with yourself and say, "A part of me would like to do thus-and-so but a bigger part of me is too lazy to try." With that level of honesty you can avoid drifting into La La Land.

Sometimes the things you would do are blocked by other forces. More often than not the stronger blocking forces are in yourself. It is reported that Abraham Lincoln often said "Some day I shall be President." He also lost eight elections before he got there. No doubt some thought he was dreaming to think he could become President. But he also said, "I will prepare and some day my chance will come." He avoided the train to La La Land and put his fantasy about being President into preparation. You know he got there. And he died there early in his second term.

A Pew Research study showed that of young people between the ages of 18 and 25, 81% rate their top goal as to get rich. 51% want to be famous. Good luck with that. But amazingly 31% believe they will some day be famous. How will we ever have time to keep track of all those rich and famous people? A few of them will pay the price to get to fame and fortune. Most will glide along the La La Land zipline wire until they hit a tree. You know they will hit that tree soon enough. Then they can start to get real.

How about you? If you haven't got something to do today that may contribute to the dream of your life, you might just be on the zipline to La La Land.

If your dream just makes you feel good but doesn't actually point to the betterment of others, you might just be on the zipline to La La Land.

If your dream doesn't include those to whom you have lifelong responsibility you are definitely on the zipline to La La Land.

If you have been putting off working on your big dream because you have to keep all the wheels of life rolling and can't get around to doing a little bit every day or at least every week then you are approaching La La Land. Get off that wire and find a better way.

What do I plan for today that will slowly but surely move me toward the grand vision I have for my life? How could I prove from the Bible that this is a worthy destination?

"The dogmas of the quiet past are inadequate to the stormy present. The occasion is piled high with difficulty, and we must rise with the occasion. As our case is new, so we must think anew and act anew." Abraham Lincoln

37

Dwelling on the Past

Whenever one leaves security, albeit associated with sadness and emptiness, and embarks on a new adventure, there needs to be a readiness to let go of old comforts. Making the physical transition is one thing. The mental is another.

The descendants of Abraham, Isaac, and Jacob, otherwise known as the Hebrew people, were miserable. They were slaves existing in Egypt, driven by taskmasters to build another man's kingdom. Their lives were boring filled with meaningless routine. They wanted out. They cried out to God for change. God heard their cry. Their moment came.

God worked over Pharaoh's heart through a series of plagues until he surrendered,

> *"Up, leave my people, you and the Israelites. Go, worship the Lord as you have requested." (Exodus 12:31)*

Moses and the Hebrews abandoned their lives of bondage. When they came to the Red Sea with Pharaoh's armies hot on their tail due to the king's regret, they took a dry plunge. God parted the sea and they trekked across on firm land. Looking over their shoulders, they watched as God wrapped the waves of water back over the Egyptian army.

Imagine the experience. Like an athletic team reliving each moment in the dressing room after the game, the stories were told with delight. "Did you see the looks on the Egyptian's faces when the water began to arch back over them?" "Yeah, I swear I saw a shark hovering just behind the wall of water when we first stepped down." "That was so cool when the lead chariot wheel jammed in mud and the driver was thrown headfirst." "My heart was pumping so hard, I thought it was going to jump out of my chest."

God supernaturally guided them through this major life transition—pillar of fire by night and a pillar of smoke by day. God was with them! Sadly, while the people themselves had physically left Egypt, they continued to operate with a slave mentality. They were prone to grumbling and complaining. At the very moment they experienced hunger or thirst pangs they murmured with discontent. They needed to simply ask God (Jehovah Jireh) to make provision for them. Though God did supply them with sweet water, quail for meat, and manna for bread, they reminisced that at least in Egypt they had rabbit food,

"We remember the fish we ate in Egypt at no cost—also the cucumbers, melons, leeks, onions and garlic." (Numbers 11:5)

It would have been better to die in Egypt than in the desert they protested.

This moment in history is a wonderful metaphor for all of us who take hold of God's perfect peace and make a courageous life change, putting our own Egypt behind us. God goes with us, leading from the front, protecting from behind, and surprising us with provisions necessary for our journey. The Hebrews, however, didn't make the mental shift. This is a danger we must be careful to avoid.

When we transition from an unhappy circumstance to something new and challenging, we must align our thought processes with our new situation. The Israelites needed to think like free men and women. They were no longer slaves. They needed to let go of old Egyptian comforts and find security in the unique and creative interventions of God. Instead of grumbling, they needed to ask God to provide their needs, trusting that He would!

The wounds people carry due to emotional, physical, and sexual abuse are deep. In order to survive, they developed coping mechanisms. Good for them! They are survivors. We are not affirming choices to use alcohol, drugs, or other addictive vices to deaden pain. We are recognizing, none the less, that the pain is real and affirming their will to cope! Some people build a relational wall around themselves complete with a bitter, angry, grumbling and sarcastic personality. They do this to keep anyone from getting too close and hurting them again.

God's redemptive plan is full. If allowed, He plans to bring healing to each of us in body, soul, and spirit, through and through. The only alternative is to personally find a way to cope with the pain. Unfortunately, those coping mechanisms sabotage the fullness of life and the thrill of new adventures. The past is permitted to poison the present.

It doesn't have to be that way. If the past is poisoning your present get some help. There is no shame in admitting the need for help. With a wise counsellor who is saturated with the Word of God and the hope He gives, you will find a way to minimize the toxic presence of the pain of the past so that you can face today and tomorrow with abounding energy and direction.

Honestly now, do I need professional help to overcome my past? What expense can I suspend in my life so I can get the real help I need?

> *"Experience is a wonderful thing; it enables you to recognize a mistake when you make it again." Unknown*

38
Making the Wrong Jump

They egg you on. You stand there with everyone saying, "C'mon jump!"

I (Gary) watched my brother-in-law with a group of teenagers. The teens were jumping off a high cliff into deep water. The kids just walked up to the cliff denying their fear and jumped. They knew that diving was the greater risk so they jumped feet first into the water straight as a knife. It was fun!

For Jim, my brother-in-law, it was different. He approached the edge of the cliff and stood there in fear for what seemed like an eternity. Then he sort of jumped and sort of slipped off the edge. But he was leaning backwards just a bit. In a failed effort to restraighten he pulled his knees up to a partial cannonball. When he hit the water he broke his back. The good news is he recovered in time and now it is just a funny memory. But it wasn't funny at the time. Everyone was quite capable of second guessing his choice to climb that cliff after it didn't work out.

Hindsight adds perspective. But the thing is you have to make your decisions going forward. We have all watched people make bad choices to end up in a wreck.

Bear this in mind, if you don't put yourself in the place where you might make a bad choice you are much better off. Never see how close to the cliff edge you can come even if you don't think you would ever jump.

Not all choices that turn out bad are sinful. Some are just stupid. Some are ill informed. With some choices there is an unforeseen bend in the cable that nobody could have expected. The choice only looks bad in the rear view mirror. But it is impossible to predict the future.

Some choices are just sinful. Sin is really sneaky. It speaks into your soul and tells you you can look into the glass case without buying the desert. It tells you that fantasy is harmless. You can imagine the taste of the sinful delight without actually experiencing it. So says sin and temptation. Casting Crowns put it this way in *Slow Fade*.

> "Be careful little eyes what you see
> It's the second glance that ties your hands as darkness pulls the strings
> Be careful little feet where you go
> For it's the little feet behind you that are sure to follow

It's a slow fade when you give yourself away
It's a slow fade when black and white have turned to gray
Thoughts invade, choices are made, a price will be paid
When you give yourself away
People never crumble in a day
It's a slow fade, it's a slow fade ...
Oh be careful little eyes what you see
Oh be careful little eyes what you see
For the Father up above is looking down in love
Oh be careful little eyes what you see."

The lesson is to make up your mind never to start down a road when you know there is big trouble down there. Others may think you narrow and bound up by imposed rules. When you self-impose the discipline it doesn't really matter what they think. Just don't follow the crowd when the crowd wants to take you too close to danger.

George Chuvalo is Canada's most famous boxer. Neither George Foreman nor Joe Frazier could knock him out. He didn't beat either of them but he did get to the big championship fights. After Foreman mauled Chuvalo round after round the referee stopped the fight and declared a technical knock out. Chuvalo said to the ref, "What are you, nuts?" Chuvalo was tough.

But he endured the heavier pain of tragedy. He lost two sons to drug overdoses and another son to suicide. His wife also took her own life. His analysis seems incredible to some. He says it starts with smoking. His thesis is that the teenager who smokes is the one at the party who will take the first drink. Then the one who drinks will take the first puff of a recreational drug. It is those who take a puff on a reefer who eventually try harder drugs until they are in the ugly grip. Many like his sons see no options. This is a slow fade.

Sadly, the Gospel didn't penetrate the Chuvalo family and stop the fight before it was too late. But you can learn right now to take a different zipline.

What are the fences I have built around my life
to protect me from making bad choices?

I. The Thrill

A. The Analogy What a zipline has to do with life.

B. The Fear Exploring the pressures to avoid the jump.

C. The Changes Adopting a readiness for something new.

D. The Start Finding the place and the team.

E. The Dream Visioning a specific life direction.

F. The Options Surveying all the possibilities.

G. The Lull Recognizing a slow down.

H. The Stall Handling the breakdowns.

I. The Thrill Experiencing the exhilaration.

J. The Ride Taking it as it comes.

K. The Awe Watching God in action.

"Life is an adventure in forgiveness." Norman Cousins

39
Choosing Adventure

When you find your ride on a particular zipline slowing down it is time to recalibrate. Maybe you just need some lubricant or even a different ride. But what you definitely require is more exhilaration in your life. The advice given by most people who seem to have accomplished something on this planet is consistent. They almost all say they would take more risks earlier in life if they had to do it over again. But of course they only got one ride.

Does a person need to know first what they are jumping into? For example, should you have another job before you resign your present job? There are many opinions on this. From a Biblical perspective the answer is quite evident. Of Abram we read in the Biblical letter to the Hebrews,

> *"By faith Abraham, when called to go to a place he would later receive as his inheritance, obeyed and went, even though he did not know where he was going." (Hebrews 11:8)*

Abram didn't have a clue where God was taking him. What he did have is trusting faith! God was testing Abram and he in turn obeyed the One who pointed the way. Every one of us will face a challenge like this. We will be called to make a jump. The discovery of what we are jumping into comes later. The wisdom is proverbial,

> *"A man's steps are directed by the LORD. How then can anyone understand his own way?" (Proverbs 20:24)*

This is not an excuse to make reckless choices without concern for those who rely on us. However, it is a reminder that when God furnishes us with a perfect peace to make a jump, all we need to really know is that God Himself is trustworthy.

Many people assume that becoming a Christian will be very much like their present life without the fun. It is just the opposite! The Christian life can be summed up with three compelling words that each person desperately needs to feel fully alive. The first is Relationship. That is a relationship with God through Jesus Christ and meaningful relationships with other people. The second is Celebration. Our life is meant to be a celebration of God's goodness and creativity. The third is Adventure. When Jesus says, "Follow me," He has in mind a life that blows mediocrity away.

According to Webster's Dictionary, an adventure involves "an exciting or remarkable experience." It is derived from the Latin "advenire" meaning to arrive. How will you ever reach the destination of becoming all that God wants you to be, unless you embrace the adventure beyond your little safe world? Chuck Swindoll noted that it is the deep things in life that are the most alluring—deep space, deep caves, and deep seas for example. The depths invite exploration. Similarly, we are called to an adventure that explores the depths of God and what it means to live according to His will. It is only when we play it safe that life turns grey. It is only when we refuse to make those necessary jumps that we waste years.

Every follower of Christ is called to a life of unconditional trust in God. This is so much more than nominal involvement in church. However, if you are experiencing nominal involvement in church it should be your first clue that you aren't experiencing that unconditional trust. After all Jesus died for His church and in your unconditional trust you follow His lead.

"... Christ loved the church and gave himself up for her ..." (Ephesians 5:25)

There are only a few reasons to stay away from deep commitment to a local church. Sometimes people make a commitment to something else and it squeezes the church out. Church is sometimes messy because people don't always follow the path you like. That is just like democracy but the difference is you might not be willing to quit and find another country. At times trust is broken in church. Countless people drop out when they see some leader or group fail miserably in a church. When people leave even for a little while it is hard to get them back in.

However, when you suck up the pain and go wall-to-wall with your local church commitment it is a stimulating adventure that gives you the arena to express your unconditional trust in God. The adventure might not always feel as such but when you look back you will be amazed at how much of an adventure you have experienced along the way!

Decide to explore the adventure of riding with Jesus down the church zipline. That is one ride you will not regret when you reach the final destination.

***What does my relationship with my church tell me
about my relationship with my Lord?***

*"If we have no peace, it is because
we have forgotten that we belong to each other." Mother Teresa*

40
Measuring Peace

It is never time to jump until you experience what the Bible terms "perfect peace." Some people use the term "gut instinct," but that term does not really capture the certainty the Holy Spirit gives a person when contemplating significant change.

> *"And the peace of God, which transcends all understanding, will guard your hearts and your minds in Christ Jesus." (Philippians 4:7)*

Imagine you are thrust so deep into water that you do not know the way to the surface. The best way to determine the direction to swim is to be still and wait for buoyancy to take affect. The moment you feel that tug, then swim with all your might in that direction. Once you experience God's "perfect peace" in your inner being, it's time to jump.

> *"Let the peace of Christ rule in your heart." (Colossians 3:15)*

In looking into this concept of perfect peace as described by Paul in Philippians you need to look at the whole context. The promise is built on some character issues.

> *"Rejoice in the Lord always. I will say it again: Rejoice! Let your gentleness be evident to all. The Lord is near. Do not be anxious about anything, but in every situation, by prayer and petition, with thanksgiving, present your requests to God." (Philippians 4:4-6)*

There are some details about how to do that in those verses. Then following that promise you can plainly see that the promise is built into a framework of proper thinking, not tranquil emotions. Paul says,

> *"... whatever is true, whatever is noble, whatever is right, whatever is lovely, whatever is admirable—if anything is excellent or praiseworthy—think about such things. Whatever you have learned or received or heard from me, or seen in me—put it into practice. And the God of peace will be with you." (Philippians 4:8-9)*

Peace isn't automatic if you just pray about your decision. You have to be living the life God has called you to live in thought and action. You can't just sit around while you decide; you must think and act the right way. If you have a problem in knowing what that is, check out the life and words of Paul. He wrote half the New Testament. Get busy.

Read Luke's account in Acts that includes biographical data about Paul and you will get plenty of clues about how to live while you are waiting.

The discipline to determine the right change for your life must start with the foundation of what God has spoken—not what you think might be a good idea. Many people make the mistake of ripping open the Scriptures to fit their preconceived desire in there. It is all too easy to see what you want to see in the Word. The point is that you must form your values out of the Word and make decisions consistent with what God said a very long time ago. His wisdom has never been rescinded and it doesn't need to be revised. You simply need to follow it.

Where did anyone ever get the idea that if you follow God's plan He will ruin your fun? Take a look around you. The people who laugh the most, have the brightest smile and the springiest step are those who are deep into following God's plan. God's plan is not just good for God; it's really good for you!

When you make the correct change for your life it is highly likely it is going to take you in a zigzag path which won't necessarily always feel like it is going in the correct direction. There will be times when you have made the correct choices and you feel like you are crossing the Sahara on foot. Every day on the correct zipline doesn't necessarily feel good. In fact, part of God's plan is that you are called to suffer.

> *"... if you suffer for doing good and you endure it, this is commendable before God. To this you were called, because Christ suffered for you, leaving you an example, that you should follow in his steps." (1 Peter 2:20-21)*

You want to be very sure that you are suffering for the right things. Suffering in life is not optional. If you haven't had a season of suffering yet, you will. How you handle that time in your life will reveal what you are truly made of.

You can have absolute confidence that you will make the right decision if you qualify for the peace dividend promised in the Word. Young or old you can make strong decisions and move out with God. Now that sounds like ziplining, doesn't it?

Do I know what it is to have peace in a storm?
What evidence would others see in me that I have that perfect peace?

41
Living Joy

Have you ever wondered why the words of Jesus about complete joy and abundant life have escaped your experience? Perhaps it's because you have been living in the bushes observing the Christian faith, not getting onto the zipline. At what point will your theology become your biography? Are you willing to go deep? Every person's life is turned by a few landmark jump moments. What is it you need to change? Is it time to add experience to your testimony?

> *"Trust in the LORD with all your heart and lean not on your own understanding; in all your ways acknowledge him, and he will make your paths straight." (Proverbs 3:5-6)*

The most challenging word in this guiding wisdom is the word "all." Dallas Willard puts it this way, "Am I a disciple or only a Christian by current standards?" His point is that a disciple does not follow Christ halfheartedly but obeys and trusts God fully. Kosuke Koyama in *No Handle on the Cross* wrote, "A man does carry the cross as he carries his briefcase." The foremost evidence of a disciple is the willingness and effort to trust God with all their heart.

> *"'For I know the plans I have for you,' declares the LORD, 'plans to prosper you and not to harm you, plans to give you hope and a future.'"*
> *(Jeremiah 29:11)*

These words are tied to His character. You will only know whether His promise and His faithfulness are trustworthy if you rely on Him with all your heart and make the necessary jump.

Twenty years from now you will be more disappointed by the things you didn't do than by the ones you did do.

> "So throw off the bowlines. Sail away from the safe harbor. Catch the trade winds in your sails. Explore. Dream. Discover." Mark Twain

Those who downhill ski know that there comes a moment when you have to push off. Those who sky dive only experience the thrill by falling forward. Those who are hooked to the zipline must lift their feet and trust the cable.

Feelings of joy or even euphoria come when certain chemicals are released in the brain. This is a good thing because it is a God thing. He created the concept. But those moments can be artificially manipulated to your detriment if you don't know the appropriate boundaries. If you get bored when you don't have some stimulant, game or activity to keep the high then you feel like you have a joy deficiency. Some people feel they are insignificant or less than fully alive unless the adrenaline is coursing through their system. When they finally slow down they feel boredom or depression. Adrenaline—or more technically epinephrine—is the hormone that serves as a stimulant in the body. It increases blood pressure and heart rate.

Epinephrine gets you ready to "go" and handle stressors in life. You need it. But you also need to relax without becoming bored or depressed. If you have a hard time with turning off the flow, it is a dead giveaway that something is amiss. Boredom is a kind of criticism of the current state you are in. There are strong links amongst boredom, depression and anger. You get angry when your goals, plans, wishes or ideas are blocked or frustrated. Joy and anger don't live at the same address. There won't be all the deep joy you want and need if you skirt the issue and pump up the hormones to avoid dealing with the underlying issues.

Sometimes you should let it all go for a while and chill. If you are feeling the need to play another sport or watch another movie on a consistent basis and that involvement cancels out the more important values of your life, you need to do some thinking about how you got into this dark place.

The joy of following the perfect leader runs much deeper than those special moments of chemical release. When the stimulation is gone and His joy is present in your life, you have a deep seated joy. Even in the middle of absolute chaos you know there is an undergirding presence. The Holy Spirit dwells inside you if you really know Jesus. This is a mystery but it isn't a fantasy.

If you aren't nodding your head in agreement with the preceding paragraph, why not? Perhaps you need to set aside the overwhelming cares of your life and read His Word. Listen as you read. Then talk to Him. Pay attention as the tension melts and the joy starts to flow again.

He is right there waiting to fill you again.

When I don't get my own way what do I do to retreat and feel better? Is that the best use of my resources? Is it sin?
Will I come out the other side a better person?

42
Colouring Life Yellow

Grey was once the colour of my (Doug's) life. Perhaps you are wondering what the colour of my life is these days. Here is the whimsical view from Dr. Seuss' book entitled *My Many Colored Days*. I like it.

"Some days are yellow. Some are blue. On different days I'm different too.
You'd be surprised how many ways I change on different colored days.
On bright red days how good it feels to be a horse and kick my heels!
On other days I'm other things. On bright blue days I flap my wings.
Some days of course, feel sort of brown. Then I feel slow and low, low down.
Then comes a yellow day. And wheeee I am a busy, buzzy bee.
Gray day…Everything is gray. I watch. But nothing moves today.
Then all of a sudden I', a circus seal! On my orange days that's how I feel.
Green days. Deep, deep in the sea. Cool and quiet fish. That's me.
On purple days I'm sad. I groan. I drag tail. I walk alone.
But when my days are happy pink it's great to jump and just not think.
Then comes my Black days. Mad. And loud. I howl. I growl at every cloud.
Then comes a mixed-up day. And wham! I don't know who or what I am!
But it all turns out all right, you see. And I go back to being me."

Do you remember my submarine dream? It was grey and claustrophobic. But God used it to actuate a better plan in real life.

I jumped from my submarine. While it was the scariest thing I ever did, it was also the most exhilarating. The grey is long gone! I have learned by experience that God is as good as His Word.

On a separate occasion, I dreamed I was driving a school bus. Not only was it empty, it was falling apart. I looked into the rearview mirror and it fell off. I tried to change gears and the clutch was so worn that the transmission ground and the bus jerked with every brutal shift. As I turned into a parking lot it took every bit of muscle I could muster to crank the wheel. Finally I got the bus parked. Exhausted I pulled the lever to open the door. It felt like the mechanisms had never been greased. The door reluctantly surrendered as I stepped off the bus and I felt relieved. As I looked across the parking lot there it was—a brand new yellow bus waiting for me.

I woke up!

It is awesome when you get it right. When you have a deep confidence that you are in the centre of God's will at this moment, you experience the tranquility deep down underneath all the present uncertainty. The future will always loom as unknown. If the greased pulleys on the secure line seem to be working for you today it is easier to forget the possibility that a branch may leave a big welt tomorrow. Certainly you can take precautions to minimize some of the future risks. And without a doubt you will usually feel like you don't have time for another crisis tomorrow. But today can you sing Johnny Nash's song because you have it right?

> "I can see clearly now, the rain is gone,
> I can see all obstacles in my way
> Gone are the dark clouds that had me blind
> It's gonna be a bright (bright), bright (bright)
> Sun-Shiny day."

Giving in to fear and oppression is never a good choice. Some fears are well-placed and should be heeded. When the vision for your life comes into better focus no fear should be sufficient to keep you from jumping on the zipline.

Look. You know this. If Jesus doesn't come back before this happens you are going to die some day. It could be sooner than you think. What makes you think you are going on unendingly on this planet? You won't live very long here before you come into contact with some person who reached a so-called untimely death. You too have an expiry date.

Let the fear of the day of reckoning you will inevitably face dominate all other fears. When you do that you won't be paralyzed by the fear; you will be energized beyond the petty fears so that you can become all you were meant to be while there is still time.

Am I focussing on being all I can be for today?
Am I doing all I can do to reach a brighter day for tomorrow?

> *"Therefore do not worry about tomorrow, for tomorrow will worry about itself. Each day has enough trouble of its own."*
> **Jesus: Matthew 6:34**

43
Enjoying the Present

Jesus instructed all who would dare to live life like Him not to worry about tomorrow. Live in the moment. As you transition from your own experience of an Egypt to a promised place, expect a wilderness-in-between-place as part of the journey. Anticipate a season of disorientation and embrace it as a unique season to trust and experience God at previously unexplored levels.

In terms of dealing with the pain of your past, recognize that while temporary coping mechanisms were helpful for a season, they will not let you move forward without pulling you back again. It's time to take the advice of Solomon who wrote,

> *"The purposes of a man's heart are deep waters, but a man of understanding draws them out." (Proverbs 20:5)*

Therapists are especially equipped to help people with this part of the journey. As you experience the reality of the Scripture concerning the crucified Christ, the cycle of insanity you have been caught in will be broken.

> *"Surely he took up our infirmities and carried our sorrows, yet we considered him stricken by God, smitten by him, and afflicted. But he was pierced for our transgressions, he was crushed for our iniquities; the punishment that brought us peace was upon him, and by his wounds we are healed." (Isaiah 53:4-5)*

Like Paul, we need to deal with the past so we can press forward to the place God has called us to.

> *"Brothers and sisters, I do not consider myself yet to have taken hold of it. But one thing I do: Forgetting what is behind and straining toward what is ahead..." (Philippians 3:13)*

God's word further instructs us:

> *"Forget the former things; do not dwell on the past. See, I am doing a new thing! Now it springs up; do you not perceive it? I am making a way in the desert and streams in the wasteland." (Isaiah 43:18-19)*

Having put the past and the future in perspective, we can focus on the delights of the present. Don't miss the thrill! Feel the wind on your face!

Van Morrison expresses it in poetic fashion:

"When will I ever learn to live in God?
When will I ever learn?
He gives me everything I need and more
When will I ever learn?
You brought it to my attention that everything was made in God
Down through the centuries of great writings and painting
Everything lives in God
Seen through architecture and great cathedrals
Down through the history of time
Is and was in the beginning and evermore shall be
Whatever it takes to fulfill His mission
That is the way we must go
But you've got to do it your own way
Tear down the old, bring up the new
And up on the hillside it's quiet
Where the shepherd is tending his sheep
And over the mountains and the valleys
The countryside is so green
Standing on the highest hill with a sense of wonder
You can see everything is made in God
Head back down the roadside and give thanks for it all
When will I ever learn to live in God?
When will I ever learn?"

Here is one technique you can use to make every day as enjoyable as it can be. In those dreary moments as you wake up in the morning and you can't think of what day it is or what you are supposed to be doing, seize the moment! That is the moment to grab your mind and wrestle it into submission. In your quietness, even if you don't feel fully rested, talk to the Lord and thank Him for the day. Make a positive confession to Him about all the good things you can force your brain into remembering. This is not the time for a 911 call to heaven. Make it a "Good morning Lord!" morning and take the attitude of those few moments with you the rest of the day.

> *How am I going to reshape my morning routines and habits*
> *to shake myself into the most beautiful "me" I can be?*

J. The Ride

A.	The Analogy	What a zipline has to do with life.
B.	The Fear	Exploring the pressures to avoid the jump.
C.	The Changes	Adopting a readiness for something new.
D.	The Start	Finding the place and the team.
E.	The Dream	Visioning a specific life direction.
F.	The Options	Surveying all the possibilities.
G.	The Lull	Recognizing a slow down.
H.	The Stall	Handling the breakdowns.
I.	The Thrill	Experiencing the exhilaration.
J.	**The Ride**	**Taking it as it comes.**
K.	The Awe	Watching God in action.

44

Checking the Equipment

By now you are living in the metaphor of the zipline. Even the cover of the book is putting you in the picture. It's that time to check to make sure everything is perfectly in place—at least as perfectly as you can assess before you jump.

So let's do a quick review.

The first thing to do is make sure you are aligned with Scripture. This must not be an alignment with just a few verses you chose to suit your purposes. It must be in accordance with the whole counsel of God. Think deeply about this. Did Jesus tell the truth? He said He did. Since He said your zipline ride would be better if you align yourself with Him what good reasons can you come up with to suggest you have better ideas? Let's be clear, a better ride is not necessarily a more comfortable ride. In fact, Jesus himself said,

> *"I have told you these things, so that in me you may have peace. In this world you will have trouble. But take heart! I have overcome the world."*
> *(John 16:33)*

This isn't a book about the words of Jesus but it is one that takes into consideration what He really said. You must too. And then of course, the rest of the Bible has relevant perspectives for you to respond to as well.

It is interesting to note that most people have some opinion about the quality of life Jesus lived. They look fondly up at Him as the ideal specimen of humanity. In fact, they might be prepared to wax eloquent about all of His personal characteristics and activities. The astounding thing is that people are prepared to do this without ever having read one word of the four Gospels that give us the facts. You have to actually study the life of Christ in order to have a valid opinion about how He might behave in your circumstances.

Secondly, examine the equipment. Your family, no matter how small, is part of your equipment. It doesn't mean you will always do exactly as your family of origin prefers. But you must consider their position and how you are going to accommodate them. In terms of the family in your household you must find a way to meet all of their needs before you make a major move.

Thirdly, check back with all of the people you consulted and ask for input into your decision. It is always best to do this before you make your final choice. Meet with them once again and describe the conclusion you are leaning toward. Make sure that they have not uncovered another factor that might delay your choice or change it. You don't want to be put in a situation where they say to you, "I wish you had talked to me because ..." This is not a meeting to simply declare your decision. While that would be appreciated to some degree because those confidants don't deserve to be the last to know, giving them a final opportunity for input makes more sense.

If you are facing a major change in your life do your best to take a deep breath before you jump. You might have the opportunity of a vacation and that would be beneficial. But generally speaking you will just need to slow the pace of life down a notch. You will be amazed as to how your sense of well being will improve if you simply get 20 minutes more sleep a night. Take this as an opportunity to clean up your sloppy habits. You want to finish well. Make sure you have forgiven any grievances you have with others in your environment. Life is way too short to take such baggage along on your new trip. You will accumulate quite enough baggage in your new context to keep you weighed down.

Recognize that whenever you move on you are going to leave some awkward moments, tense conversations and failures behind. If your conscience is bothering you so much that you need to have the conversation before you jump, you had better have that conversation. There will never be a better time than right now. Think through exactly what you need to say and leave everything else unsaid. Have you ever met anyone who benefited by taking a few parting shots? Probably not. Leave that for someone else to cover in the future. And in the end of the day make sure you rest in this truth,

"It is mine to avenge; I will repay..." (Deuteronomy 32:35)

Tidy up your outfit. Put on a clean shirt if you need to—make it a bright one! Brush your teeth. Comb your hair. Climb into the harness. Straighten your helmet. Readjust the Velcro on your gloves. Snap on to that line—there are two snaps you know. Smile. Never let them see you sweat. Just jump!

Do I really take all the people I should into consideration? Or would I rather sneak past the decision so I can get my own way and worry about the consequences later?

> *"The human heart is like a ship on a stormy sea driven about
> by winds blowing from all four corners of heaven." Martin Luther*

45
Freezing on the Edge

Robert C. O'Brien, in *Mrs. Frisby and the Rats of NIMH*, captures how the accumulation of things squeezes the simplicity and joy out of lives. The story was about a woman in a small town who bought a vacuum cleaner. Her name was Mrs. Jones and until then she, like all her neighbours, had kept the house spotlessly clean by using a broom and a mop. But the vacuum cleaner did it faster and better! Mrs. Jones was the envy of all the other housewives in town so they bought vacuum cleaners too.

The vacuum cleaner business became very brisk. In fact the company that made them opened a branch factory in the town. The factory used a lot of electricity, of course, along with the women with their vacuum cleaners. The electric power company had to put up a big new plant to keep them all running. In its furnaces the power plant burned coal and out of its chimneys black smoke poured all day and night, blanketing the town with soot and making all the floors dirtier than ever. Still, by working twice as hard and twice as long, the women of the town were able to keep their floors almost as clean as they had been before Mrs. Jones ever bought a vacuum cleaner in the first place.

We do make things hard for ourselves sometimes. Most of us are like the old man carrying a heavy load. The driver of a caribou wagon was on his way to market when he overtook this burdened man. Taking compassion on him, the driver invited him to ride in the wagon. Gratefully, the traveller accepted. After a few minutes, the driver turned to see how the man was doing. To his surprise, he found him still straining under the heavy weight. He had not taken the burden off his shoulders.

Jesus said,

> *"Come to me, all you who are weary and burdened, and I will give you rest."*
> *(Matthew 11:28)*

God does not want us to carry unnecessary burdens. In many cases, the weariness comes from attempting to sustain a lifestyle based on the things that money can buy. Don't get this wrong, money is a pretty fair servant but it is a terrible master. You won't find a full life by filling more garages with toys.

Really, you don't need the shiniest new electronic toy to put in your pocket to show all

---

your friends in the school yard. That might make them all jealous and give you an opportunity to gloat. But it comes with a long term contract and next week someone will come out with one that is better. Your bragging rights will run out a long time before the contract does.

> *"Therefore, since we are surrounded by such a great cloud of witnesses, let us throw off everything that hinders and the sin that so easily entangles, and let us run with perseverance the race marked out for us. Let us fix our eyes on Jesus, the author and perfecter of our faith, who for the joy set before him endured the cross, scorning its shame, and sat down at the right hand of the throne of God. Consider him who endured such opposition from sinful men, so that you will not grow weary and lose heart." (Hebrews 12:1-3)*

What is stopping you from letting go of those things you cannot really trust instead of free falling into God's arms? Are you trying to feel secure and safe inside? Charlie Peacock, in his song *Monkeys at the Zoo* wrote,

> "No amount or green, gold, or silver,
> The perfect body, another hot toddy,
> Work for the Lord, fame & power, power and sex,
> A seat at a table at the Belle Meade Country Club..."

Here's the rub—nothing will ever take the place of the peace of God.

In another song, *William and Maggie*, he wrote,

> "Oh, it always amazed me how someone could come to the edge of the world, drop a stone down the side and turn and return to the very same life."

Why do so many people come to the edge of necessary change and refuse to make the jump? A child might freeze at the edge of a swimming pool or at the end of a dock for a variety of reasons. Fear of drowning is the most obvious answer. As the Bible indicates, fear is overcome by love. When a parent is there with arms wide open to encourage and catch them, bravery rises up. Eventually the child will jump.

It is hard to make any kind of jump without the encouragement and support of someone else. People change in the context of relationship with others. Moses instructed Joshua to *"Be strong and courageous."* As Joshua prepared to make the jump into the promised land, he did so with Caleb by his side. This is one of the benefits of having a personal Life Coach. You may know that there is no better time to make the jump. Your Coach will help you with the courage. Ultimately, if it is the right jump, God will not let you fall.

> *Do I need to find a good Life Coach to help me through this next jump? If I don't hire a Coach who will be there to save me from wasting months or years I can never recapture?*

"Hindsight explains the injury that foresight
would have prevented." Unknown

46
Looking Back

Immediately after you take the jump you might find yourself exclaiming, "What have I done?" But don't dwell too long on that question because you will be in big trouble if you don't watch where you are going much more than you look back to where you have come from.

If you do your work in advance you are much less likely to ever draw the conclusion that you made the wrong jump. Once you have jumped you will realize that your new circumstance isn't as perfect as it looked before you jumped. As you move further and further down the line you will discover more and more the implications of your choices. If you truly find yourself in a mess you either have to clean up the mess or get out of it. Regretting that you made the choice in the first place won't help you now.

Sometimes you need to repent. Repentance is a change of mind with a resulting change of life. If you are too proud to repent when you need to, you are going to grind your zipline ride to a halt. Ask yourself if you are of such a disposition that you could admit it if you are really wrong. Don't be too quick at this. Think of times in your life when you have already turned around and others around you who know you best would confirm that you actually did so. A pastor asked a former pastor of his church if there ever was a time when he did something for which he needed to apologize. The man thought deeply and said, "I don't believe I've ever had such a time in my life." You guessed it. Everyone else around him could reference multiple such opportunities. But he was so lacking in self awareness that he couldn't see. Since that is not where you want to end up, make sure that you are truly prepared to repent when it is called for.

You must make the best of the situation. Don't be grumpy about how wrong other people were in either telling you to jump or not telling you the whole truth about what would happen if you did. Get out a big piece of chalk. Put a big mark in the experience column. But don't get bitter about it. All you have to do is change one letter to move from bitter to better.

There will be times when you make a bad jump. But you will have the opportunity to learn from that. Some find it hard to believe, but God always leaves room for you to begin again. You don't get to go back and start over. But you always have the opportunity to start again. The resources available in time, talent and treasure may be diminished but there is always enough to start again.

When things don't go as you wish the emotional tendency is to dwell upon what is going wrong. You definitely have to think about what is going wrong in order to define a better future. If you burn up too much emotional fuel on the process you won't have anything left for the next day. Looking back is only useful to the extent that you can take out of your awareness information, factors and elements that will help you for the next leg of your journey.

Have you ever noticed how long contracts tend to get? A deal starts off with a handshake over a barrel head. Then it grows into a modest handwritten document of agreement. Then someone suggests you need to have a lawyer to look it over. Hah! They never just look it over. They recommend 14 pages of amendments. Of course your lawyer adds his 14 pages to cover your interests and that creates an imbalance so the document goes back to the other side were the other lawyer, not to be outdone, adds 17 pages of amendments. You might actually get your deal done. But the reality is if your deal goes straight south you have probably lost all your time and at least most of your money regardless of the length of the original agreement. Time is the most valuable commodity you have on your zipline. Don't waste your time. You can never recapture what was lost. You could get some money but what good is that when measured against your bigger loss?

The question always is, "What are we going to do now?" If you are still bickering over how you got to where you are your lenses will be all fogged up. You cannot see clearly when emotional fuel is burning. There are times when the deep hurts of life cloud your judgment. You will need a close friend, mentor, counsellor or coach to talk things through with. But you must get to that current question, "What's next for me?" Looking back has limited value.

How often do I say a sincere, "I'm sorry" without simply desiring to get off the hook? What are my first reactions when I mess up? What can I learn from my reactions?

47
Reducing Speed

One of the wisest things you can do to take full advantage of the present is to slow down. We live in a rat race and the rats keep scurrying faster. How often do we say, "Look at the time, I have to get going." An African tribe would insist on resting after an extended time of travel. They explained that this was time for their spirits to catch up to their bodies. For many of us, our bodies are so far ahead of our spirits, it will take an extended illness for them to catch up. Even on Sundays, many of us are in a hurry to get home for lunch or to do whatever is planned for the rest of day.

Hurrying is a sin to the degree that we miss divine appointments. How often do we fail to stop and converse with someone because we are preoccupied with the next thing on our agenda? We think a person stopping to talk to us on the street is an interruption. It might be the most important way we can invest our time.

Jesus told a parable about a man who was mugged on the road and left for dead. Two religious types walked by him—a priest and a Levite. They walked on the other side of the road avoiding the victim. Only a Samaritan stopped to help. Why did the other two pass by? After all, as religious people shouldn't they have been compelled to be compassionate? Perhaps they felt they didn't have the time to spare.

God has never been in a hurry to do anything.

> *"But when the fullness of the time was come, God sent forth his Son, made of a woman, made under the law." (Galatians 4:4 King James Version).*

Jesus was travelling with His disciples. Parents brought their children with the request He bless them. The disciples tried to keep the families back.

> *"People were bringing little children to Jesus for him to place his hands on them, but the disciples rebuked them. When Jesus saw this, he was indignant. He said to them, 'Let the little children come to me, and do not hinder them, for the kingdom of God belongs to such as these.'" (Mark 10:13-14)*

Jesus was travelling to the other side of Galilee for some R & R. The crowds kept following. The disciples said, "Send them away." They felt that Jesus' day timer was already full. Instead Jesus made space for the crowd and set the table for the miracle of feeding five thousand. (Mark 6:30-44)

We never see Jesus buzzing here, there, and everywhere like a fly on the window. Jesus walked on the water. Jesus walked on the earth. We are to follow in His steps.

On a very practical level, one of the things we can do to facilitate a change of pace is to reduce our wants. Most people read the advertising flyers more than their Bibles. Then they hurry off to the retail stores to purchase stuff they don't really need. In the days to follow, they whirl about to service and repair these same items. If we just reclaimed the time we spent accumulating, repairing, and storing objects, we would be wonder-filled at how much more time we have available.

We live in a very fast paced world and there is never enough time in our day to do all that we want to do. We have lost a proper sense of pacing our lives. The truth is that you can do anything you want to do but you can't do everything you want to do. Read that sentence again because if you understand it you will have discovered an old truth that can change your life right now. You can really do anything you want to do today— well almost anything. Start early and apply yourself to something. In a matter of time you can succeed. Everything has a price. After years you will reach your goal. You will look around and see others who have reached their goals also. Some appear to be more successful than you have become. They have also paid a higher price more than likely.

You often hear celebrities complain about how hard it is to bring up children today. They have plenty of money to meet all of their physical needs. Unfortunately, because they have put their careers before their families they have been absent most of the time while their kids were growing up. It is impossible to go back and re-edit that script. They have made millions but have lost their kids to drugs or rebellion. They have had to make a choice. Is it my career or is it my family? They cannot have everything. As that old expression puts it, they wanted to have their cake and eat it too.

Be sober and determine what you want. But realize you can't have everything you want. A fulfilled life, a life worth living is worthy of sacrifice. A mother or father who sacrifices a promotion in order to spend more time with their family may be criticized by others but not by their kids. The kids will rise up and call them blessed because they put their needs ahead of their own.

Fast paced living results in a loss of perspective. Our brains are overexposed today by images and messages that bombard us. They shape our thinking. We have no time to sit quietly in our room and think—not fall asleep.

Make time to think. You will not regret it.

Where is my quiet place where I can go and think without interruption?
How can I rearrange my life so I get there more often
for an appropriate duration?

48
Walking Barefoot

Moses demonstrated that he could be impulsive. He tried to defend a Hebrew who was being roughed up by an Egyptian and thus he killed the bully. To avoid the civil consequences, Moses fled into the wilderness and lived as a refugee for forty years. Meanwhile, the Hebrews continued to suffer under Egyptian power.

After all this time, Moses was tending the flock of Jethro his father-in-law, the priest of Midian. He led the flock to the far side of the desert and came to Horeb, the mountain of God. There the angel of the LORD appeared to him in flames of fire from within a bush. Moses saw that though the bush was on fire it did not burn up. So Moses thought, "I will go over and see this strange sight—why the bush does not burn up."

> *"When the LORD saw that he had gone over to look, God called to him from within the bush, 'Moses! Moses!' And Moses said, 'Here I am.' 'Do not come any closer,' God said. 'Take off your sandals, for the place where you are standing is holy ground.' Then he said, 'I am the God of your father, the God of Abraham, the God of Isaac and the God of Jacob.' At this, Moses hid his face, because he was afraid to look at God." (Exodus 3:1-7)*

Why did God compel Moses to take off his sandals? The answer is obvious, right? God told him to take off his sandals because the ground he was standing on was holy. Wasn't there a little more to it than that? After all, God appears and speaks to many people throughout the Biblical record. No where else does He instruct the individual to remove their footwear.

Many years ago I (Doug) worked at a community group home for girls. I worked the night shift. Two of us were responsible for fifteen girls between the ages of twelve and sixteen who were wards of the court. I had the sleep shift which meant that the other staff members stayed awake. However, in times of crisis I was alerted to deal with an issue at hand.

About 7 am on a cold Saturday January morning, the other childcare worker wakened me. She indicated that some of the girls were up earlier than usual and behaving oddly. I began to circulate to discern the situation and agreed that something was afoot. I assumed two of the girls were planning on bolting through the doors and running away.

I invited the two girls I suspected into the games room. I sat upon a couch. When they entered, I asked them to sit down on the other couch.

"What do you want to talk about?" they asked.

"Oh, I just thought we could have a little visit this morning. How are you girls? Did you have a good sleep? Is school going well? Wow, you are awake earlier than usual for a Saturday morning."

As I spoke with them, I could tell they were uneasy. I also noticed that they had their shoes on.

"Why do you girls have your shoes on?"

"What? We always wear our shoes in here." The tone of their voice revealed shock that I would ask such a ridiculous question.

"Really? I'll tell you what I'm thinking. I'm thinking that you two girls are planning on busting out those doors and making a run for it."

"What?" They seemed exasperated. "No. We weren't planning that."

"Okay then," I answered, "you won't mind doing something for me as an indication of good faith? Take off your shoes and give them to me until later."

They were horrified. They were offended. They were insulted. They were busted! One week later they confessed their plans to another staff member and noted that I had made them take off their shoes, making it impossible to run away on snow covered roads.

There comes a time when you need to give up your shoes in order to experience the right kind of walk. To change the imagery you can ride the zipline without the perfect safety net below. It is a far greater risk to keep faulty options open to yourself than it is to narrow the options to assure yourself that you will take the correct ride.

Can I identify some "shoes" I am clinging to that simply need to go?
How will I properly dispose of them?

> *"Security is mostly a superstition. It does not exist in nature, nor do the children of men as a whole experience it. Avoiding danger is no safer in the long run than outright exposure. Life is either a daring adventure or nothing." Helen Keller*

49
Dropping the Sandals

What do you do when you're afraid? Sometimes you run in the opposite direction! Have you ever tried to walk or run barefoot on hot beach sand? You best stand in one place and sink your feet a little deeper to keep them cool. I imagine desert sand is even hotter.

"Take off your sandals, Moses. I don't want you running away now. Take some time with me. I have something to say if you will only stop and listen."

If Moses had not stopped, taken off his sandals and stayed awhile, he would have missed God unfolding the awesome plan for his life and the Hebrew people. Are we not like blind men on galloping horses oblivious to the burning bushes all around us? We need to use the brakes. God is saying to each of us,

> *"Be still and know that I am God." (Psalm 46:10)*

Too many people approach the Ten Commandments the way they do their mid-term exam. Six out of ten is a pass. But we need to honour all of them, including the fourth which is to keep the Sabbath. Leslie Flynn came up with the term "the ten commandos" asserting that all ten were given to protect us. The principle of Sabbath rest was to abstain from that which you deemed work the other six days—to be refreshed. The alternative is eventual burnout.

God will not compete for your attention. You need to put yourself in a position to see and draw near to a burning bush. For many years I (Doug) was taught that a Christian ought to have daily devotions, a time of Bible reading and prayer. Without question, this has been and is a wonderful discipline for countless followers of Jesus. That never really worked for me though; I carried a pound of guilt every day. Then Jack Hayford made an analogy to bathing and devotions. "Which is better?" he asked. "Sprinkling yourself with a few drops every morning or having a good long soak once a week?" For me, it made sense. My rhythm has always been to chisel out an afternoon or an evening (I am not a morning person) to take extended time with God. Low lights, a little John Michael Talbot music, my Bible open, and I am camped out at a burning bush.

It is in barefoot moments the message of Psalm 23 can become your experience:

> *"The LORD is my shepherd, I shall not be in want. He makes me lie down*

in green pastures, he leads me beside quiet waters, he restores my soul. He guides me in paths of righteousness for his name's sake." (Psalm 23:1-3)

This isn't some regimented obligation. For many, daily works best. And they have found that the morning is the best time. That is when they are freshest and they know enough about themselves that if they don't get this time in early in the day other pressures will squeeze it out. If you are bent to forget the Master if you don't meet Him every morning then by all means you will sin if you miss the meeting.

The point is this, you must arrange for time to kick back and drop the sandals so you can have a meaningful meeting with God. If a week goes by and you don't do that ask yourself if you really love Him as much as you say you do. Your walk with Him should include a moment by moment awareness of His Word and a prayerful attitude. And in addition to that you need focussed time in His presence. If you have never made this your pattern then it might seem strange to you. You don't know what you are missing!

Analogies from other relationships might help. If you have a friend you love to spend time with you get together and do whatever it is you do. The time just rolls by as you are enjoying each other. If you have a child you love you know what games or treats to plan or bring home with you. That child might meet you at the door excitedly ready to play the game even though you are exhausted. You fake a smile and try to catch your second wind. Soon you are reenergized and having fun with each other again. If you know your spouse likes certain things to do or places to be you plan to go there and do those things because it is their first choice—not because it is yours. Loving relationships are not selfish relationships.

What does the Father want in His relationship with you that you can enjoy together?

"... true worshipers will worship the Father in the Spirit and in truth, for they are the kind of worshipers the Father seeks. God is spirit, and his worshipers must worship in the Spirit and in truth." (John 4:23-24)

Get those sandals off and meet with Him regularly. He will speak to you through His Word and your thoughts will move into sync with His. You can tell Him the whole story of the day detail by detail and He will never be bored or miss the complicated plot line.

Now that is the life! Enjoy it and never miss an opportunity to meet with Him.

What restructuring do I need to do to make sure I never miss an appointment with God? How will I let others know when I am in that important meeting it is no time to interrupt me?

> *"In character, in manner, in style, in all things,*
> *the supreme excellence is simplicity." Henry Wadsworth Longfellow*

50
Simplifying Life

You have made intentional efforts at simplifying your life. Good! You have incorporated devotional disciplines into your relationship with God. Super! Even though your adventure may take you through shadows and enemies will try to thwart you, God's favour will splash over the edges of your life.

> *"Even though I walk through the valley of the shadow of death, I will fear*
> *no evil, for you are with me; your rod and your staff, they comfort me. You*
> *prepare a table before me in the presence of my enemies. You anoint my head*
> *with oil; my cup overflows. Surely goodness and love will follow me all the*
> *days of my life, and I will dwell in the house of the LORD forever."*
> *(Psalm 23:4-6)*

These words are David's personal testimony—the voice of experience. Fear of the uncertainty of what's next will be overcome by God's goodness, love, guidance, and comfort.

Whenever a person purchases a new vehicle, in the days that follow, they will find themselves saying, "Hey, there's another one!" Suddenly, that person will notice how many other vehicles of the same brand, model, and colour are on the road. We see what we are looking for. Whenever you have invested some of your time with God, in the days to follow you will also begin to see Him in places you did not previously notice.

At a Vacation Bible School, the children were encouraged to write down their God sightings. What a great idea. They were encouraged to wear a God mindset and record every perceived evidence of God being present and working. This might include receiving an unexpected kindness, a direct answer to prayer, a personal message from the Bible, or even an unplanned opportunity to show care to someone else. Each of these sightings adds to the thrill of following Christ, especially into the unknown. In fact, if God could speak to Balaam through a literal ass (Numbers 22:28), don't be surprised that you hear God getting your attention from strange sources such as movies or novels. God is creative. He spoke to Moses and the Israelites through clouds and stone tablets. Without question, God will also encourage and communicate with you if you are in the frame of mind to listen to His voice.

Having said that, your mind is vulnerable to negative influencers and must be protected.

If the wheels on your vehicle have good air pressure then you will safely arrive at your destination. Let the air out of even one tire and the trip is over. Your mind along with the faith, strength, and courage necessary to press forward will deflate if negativity is allowed to puncture a hole.

Your mind can only think about one thing at a time.

By focussing on the faithfulness of God and His wonderful works as evidenced in the universe and your personal life leaves no room for negativity to steal your joy. Be careful what you watch. Be careful whom you listen to. Pray that the ...

> *"...peace of God, which transcends all understanding, will guard your hearts and your minds in Christ Jesus" (Philippians 4:7).*

One of the most significant exercises I (Doug) have done over the last twenty-five years is journal. It is an exceptional way to be made new in the attitude of one's mind. I have recorded every prayer and dated it. I have chronicled every major life changing decision and the factors that prompted it. I have written down every Scripture, dream and quote that somehow spoke to me. When I review these journals, I see from a broader perspective the trace of God's hand over my life. My conclusion is that if God has been faithful to me thus far, surely I can trust Him again.

Journaling is something to consider. If you have not started this is a good day to begin. What do you write in your journal? There are no static rules. Just write what makes sense to you. You don't have to use complete sentences unless you want to. You might set up some categories that make sense for you and see if there is something to add to each category day by day. You might want to capture quotes from others that strike a responsive chord for you. Tell your story to yourself; you will forget your story very quickly if you don't document it. And the rich value of your story will grow over time. Like looking back at photos from your past, the review of the words you wrote will have great interest and instruction for you.

If you don't have time for this kind of reflection it is time to push something out of the way and simplify your day. Be like a kid again and track those God sightings.

> ***What works for me as I document the work of God in my life?***
> ***Which mindless pattern needs to go***
> ***so I have time for a more meaningful and simple life?***

> *"The Christian life is not a constant high. I have my moments of deep discouragement. I have to go to God in prayer with tears in my eyes, and say, 'O God, forgive me.' or 'Help me.'" Billy Graham*

51
Riding out the Highs and Lows

In the midst of transition, we need to live in the present and absorb the wonders of the experience. We read about Elijah, the man of God and fiery prophet starting at 1 Kings 17. He knew about the thrill of serving God. Elijah was the one who challenged King Ahab and the prophets of Baal to a contest on Mount Carmel. It was for the purpose of demonstrating which God was true—Yahweh or Baal? When the contest was held, the altars of Baal remained absent of life or flame. In contrast, Elijah's God emitted fire from heaven to consume the sacrifice on His altar. Spectators were persuaded that Elijah's God was the one true God.

Elijah was on a mountaintop when this happened—not just in a physical sense. He was on an emotional high. This was an exhilarating encounter with God. He had many of them—when ravens fed him, when he was instrumental in the multiplication of the widow's oil and flour, when he was used to resurrect a young boy. Figuratively speaking, these were all mountaintop experiences.

But not every moment was like that. Elijah knew the valley too! Elijah, the man who collaborated with God for the demonstration of divine power sometimes slipped into discouragement. To be discouraged is to lose courage. It is a low place. It's a place where everything that is against you seems bigger.

A story is told that Satan one day organized the tools of his trade. He kept them in jars upon a shelf and on this day he was lining them up in a row.

PRIDE HATE JEALOUSY DECEIT MALICE GREED LUST SELFISHNESS

A little apart from all the others was one more jar, nearly empty.

A junior devil asked Lucifer, "Why is this one used so much?"

"Because," said the betrayer, "One pinch of that inside a man and he is mine. I can use him in any way that suits my purpose. It is so low because I have used it so much."

The jar was labeled DISCOURAGEMENT.

When you hit bottom, everything looks large and overbearing.

Just as Elijah's words highlight symptoms of discouragement and depression, God's words in response will help each of us to stay strong, courageous and not lose heart.

Life on the Zipline ~ from Fear to Awe

Through an angel, God instructed Elijah, *"Get up and eat."* (1 Kings 19:5). Here's the big point. Contributing to Elijah's emotional and psychological valley experience was the fact that he was physically exhausted and under nourished. When we let our physical bodies deplete themselves of rest and nourishment, our soul and spirits become vulnerable. The word "exhaust" means to be drawn out of. Elijah's victory on the mountain followed by the long journey into the valley desert from Jezebel left him empty.

The word HALT is a great acronym for those of us wanting to live in the present and enjoy the ride. You should not allow yourself to get hungry, angry, lonely or tired. To neglect yourself in just one of these ways will tilt you off balance and render you susceptible to distortions of reality. It would seem Elijah did just that. Instead of answering his prayer to die, God gives him some practical counsel.

The angel of the LORD says,

> *"Get up and eat, for the journey is too much for you."* (1 Kings 19:7)

Elijah needed to hear this. It's a dose of reality. God's journey is always too much for a person to go it alone.

The key is this—you will fail absolutely in your zipline ride of life if you don't walk with God. Walking with God every day is what you need. Discouragement will come but it won't dominate sufficiently to win in the end.

In the end this is the truth.

> *"What, then, shall we say in response to these things? If God is for us, who can be against us? He who did not spare his own Son, but gave him up for us all—how will he not also, along with him, graciously give us all things? Who will bring any charge against those whom God has chosen? It is God who justifies. Who then is the one who condemns? No one. Christ Jesus who died—more than that, who was raised to life—is at the right hand of God and is also interceding for us. Who shall separate us from the love of Christ? Shall trouble or hardship or persecution or famine or nakedness or danger or sword? ... No, in all these things we are more than conquerors through him who loved us. For I am convinced that neither death nor life, neither angels nor demons, neither the present nor the future, nor any powers, neither height nor depth, nor anything else in all creation, will be able to separate us from the love of God that is in Christ Jesus our Lord."* (Romans 8:31-39)

> ***The next time I feel discouraged what new technique will I use to keep myself from slipping into sin? Who in my life will help me through dark days when they come?***

K. The Awe

A. The Analogy   What a zipline has to do with life.

B. The Fear   Exploring the pressures to avoid the jump.

C. The Changes   Adopting a readiness for something new.

D. The Start   Finding the place and the team.

E. The Dream   Visioning a specific life direction.

F. The Options   Surveying all the possibilities.

G. The Lull   Recognizing a slow down.

H. The Stall   Handling the breakdowns.

I.   The Thrill   Experiencing the exhilaration.

J.   The Ride   Taking it as it comes.

K. The Awe   Watching God in action.

> *"After the earthquake came a fire, but the LORD was not in the fire. And after the fire came a gentle whisper." 1 Kings 19:12*

52
Meeting Him

Mark Wellman lives his life according to a "no limits" philosophy. In the summer of 1989, Mark earned acclaim by climbing the sheer granite face of El Capitan in Yosemite National Park. What made this event historic is that Mark is a paraplegic. His climbing companion, Mike Corbett, carried Mark on his shoulders for the seven days it took to scale El Capitan.

This is the way it is with all of us in terms of the journey God has set before us.

"For the journey is too much for you." (1 Kings 19:7)

Elijah found a cave up in a mountain and slept for the night. There God asked Elijah a question we all need to answer.

"What are you doing here Elijah?" (1 Kings 19:9)

If you are discouraged or depressed, ask yourself that same question, "What are you doing here _____?" Elijah answered God by telling Him his story of highs and lows.

In the past, Elijah's experiences with God had predominantly been encounters with supernatural manifestations. So up the mountain he went to get another power fix!

But what happened on the top of the mountain taught Elijah that nourishment for the soul and for the journey is not provided through miraculous power demonstrations. Instead, inner fuel is imparted through quiet communion with the Lord.

A great and powerful wind tore the mountain apart and shattered the rocks. When the wind had stopped, Elijah felt empty. God was not in the wind. Then came an earthquake. But when the earthquake stopped, Elijah continued to feel empty. God was not in the quake. Then came a raging fire. Trees snapped. But afterwards, Elijah still felt empty. God wasn't in the fire as he hoped.

Finally, something obscure, something unseen, yet something alive and real happened. It was like a whisper heard only on the inside, upon his spirit.

> *"The spirit of man is the candle of the LORD, searching all the inward parts of the belly." (Proverbs 20:27 King James Version)*

God was in a still small voice. It was an exchange of affection. It was more than food for the body; it was strength for the soul. Elijah had come up the mountain for a power fix, but instead found renewal in quiet fellowship with God.

> *"The LORD said, 'Go out and stand on the mountain in the presence of the LORD, for the LORD is about to pass by.' Then a great and powerful wind tore the mountains apart and shattered the rocks before the LORD, but the LORD was not in the wind. After the wind there was an earthquake, but the LORD was not in the earthquake. After the earthquake came a fire, but the LORD was not in the fire. And after the fire came a gentle whisper." (1 Kings 19:11-12)*

Elijah had lapsed into discouragement for the very same reasons we do today. He hadn't cared for himself physically, emotionally, or spiritually. The assumption that God was feeding his spirit in the demonstrations and it was enough was not true. Elijah needed more!

God gave his man some profound advice,

> *"Go back the way you came." (1 Kings 19:15)*

In other words, "Elijah, now you know why you're discouraged. Now you understand how you came to be depressed. Retrace your steps and see. Make a new beginning."

The ultimate experience is to walk humbly with God. That is to live with a clear conscience knowing that in all aspects of life, obedience is the norm and that when you become aware of sin you confess it, receive forgiveness and move on with Him. That relationship is often described in human terms because we are left without enough communication tools to describe it adequately. Hand in hand. Side by side. Walking together. As we become aware of His will for our moral and personal fabric, then live it out. The experience is rich and indescribable. It is personal.

> *"Praise be to the God and Father of our Lord Jesus Christ! In his great mercy he has given us new birth into a living hope through the resurrection of Jesus Christ from the dead, and into an inheritance that can never perish, spoil or fade. This inheritance is kept in heaven for you, who through faith are shielded by God's power until the coming of the salvation that is ready to be revealed in the last time. In all this you greatly rejoice, though now for a little while you may have had to suffer grief in all kinds of trials. These have come so that the proven genuineness of your faith—of greater worth than gold, which perishes even though refined by fire—may result in praise, glory and honor when Jesus Christ is revealed. Though you have not seen him, you love him; and even though you do not see him now, you believe in him and are filled with an inexpressible and glorious joy, for you are receiving the end result of your faith, the salvation of your souls." (1 Peter 1:3-9)*

Is my walk with God secure enough that I can perceive His gentle whisper?

53
Navigating Mountains and Valleys

In the western world we are flooded with entertainment. I (Warwick) used to love watching the coming attractions when I was a kid. Fantasizing about what might take place in the movie to arrive in my local theater the next month was almost as good as seeing the final product. It was exciting to see them. But that was then, back when they let you wonder.

Now trailers are just one tentacle of an eight-armed octopus assault of junkets, blogs, events, talk-show promotion and pre-release products—all to make sure audiences have an insane amount of information before the film even arrives. We have more information than we need at any one time. We are connected to our digital toys to the point that we aren't quite sure if we could ever walk alone down a one-lane road in the country and enjoy the breeze and flowers by the side of the road.

We need to live in this world even though it is like a busy valley, crowded with activity, events and people. We can't avoid it.

But we also need to take time apart to get up into the mountains where the air is thinner and the view is grander and the sounds are softer. We need a time away from our world so we can regain a perspective on life.

Hole Hearted is an acoustic rock song by the American group Extreme. Here are some of the relevant words.

> "Life's ambition occupies my time
> Priorities confuse the mind
> Happiness one step behind
> This inner peace I've yet to find
> This heart of stone is where I hide
> These feet of clay kept warm inside
> Day by day less satisfied
> Not fade away before I die
> If I'm not blind why can't I see
> That a circle can't fit
> Where a square should be

There's a hole in my heart
That can only be filled by you
And this hole in my heart
Can't be filled with the things I do
There's a hole in my heart
That can only be filled by you
Should have known from the start
I'd fall short with the things I do
Hole hearted
Hole hearted
Hole hearted
Hole hearted."

The writer of this song hit on the truth that everyone needs to face. There is a hole in the heart that only God can fill. People are by nature spiritual beings. We will not find our purpose or our proper passions fulfilled until we find our place in God's agenda for our lives. Socrates claimed that the unexamined life is not worth living.

If you keep your life filled with life in the valley and never take time in the mountains to understand how God fits in and you fit in with Him you will only grow old and never wiser. Life continues and we grow wise too late.

> *"You who bring good news to Zion, go up on a high mountain. You who bring good news to Jerusalem, lift up your voice with a shout, lift it up, do not be afraid; say to the towns of Judah, 'Here is your God!'" (Isaiah 40:9)*

Several times a year get out of that humid valley where the busyness consumes you. Get away somewhere where you can clear your head and relax. Go to the lake or the mountain. If you can't afford that just go to the library or the park for a day. You are not super human; you need the perspective that comes from the mountain because that is where you can best be filled by Him.

When is my next spiritually driven vacation?
When I come back what will I have accomplished?

54
Seeing What God Sees

Every human has amazing capacity. Even the least intelligent of people or most disabled still have capacity beyond what most believe. If you have ever had the opportunity to live beside a person who is facing moments leading up to death you have become aware of life in a way others cannot appreciate. The finality of a final breath is indelible and sacred. It changes everyone who lives beside it. Some get bitter. Others get better.

The life experience of living beside human death is powerful. That is probably so because humans were created in the image of God. That mysterious thought takes us to the next world. There is a next world. Every tribe and society on earth has tried to make some sense out of the next life. Most explanations are confused because they fail to build on the foundation of what God has clearly spoken in the pages of the Bible. Try as people might it is impossible to stamp out the sense that there is something more beyond the grave. It is possible with bravado to declare that death ends it all until the moment comes. The dying soul may shake its stubborn fist at the eternal but that only proves there is something eternal to confront.

> *"He has made everything beautiful in its time. He has also set eternity in the human heart; yet no one can fathom what God has done from beginning to end." (Ecclesiastes 3:11)*

It is totally unrealistic and rebellious to deny these facts. There is no point in living in denial. You must not live without reference to the meaning beyond. You are wired for eternity.

In one verse, Solomon establishes three basic truths but let's personalize them for you. Please insert your first name in the blank and meditate.

1. God is the creator of _____'s beauty and sometimes that beauty takes time to unfold.
2. _____'s heart is unchangingly religious. _____ believes in eternity.
3. _____ isn't going to figure it all out.

Now let's back up. Did you find yourself doubting any of these statements? Did you feel a little hypocritical in reciting them because there is a portion of your insides that doubts the reality of these statements or wishes they weren't true?

God, and He is a personal, communicative, intimate friend when you know Him, sees you as beautiful. He created you. He knows all about the dark parts—more than any human including yourself. But He knows what He has built within you and is your makeover partner willing to let all the beauty out as you work with Him. And it will happen over time.

God made you incurably thirsty for fulfillment that can only come from Him because He is the one who put the meaning in your inner parts. You don't yet know all the meaning in your inner parts but He does.

God is way bigger than your conception of Him. You are just not that smart. No offense. But every time you question things that are undoubtedly controlled by the hand of God you are implying that He has somehow made a goof up. Take it a step further. Every time God allows an evil person to prosper or a disaster to occur, He actually did allow it to happen. Why? Sorry. No answers here. It is unfathomable.

There are definite things we can know about the plan of God for this world. There are things you can personally learn to see that you haven't noticed until now about His intentions and desires for you. You can get in sync with those desires and plans. You can make Him the most important person in your life and encourage others to do the same. Watch as He works things out through you.

And the best part is this, you don't have to try to figure it all out! You just have to live it. He will make it all make sense at the end. During time it might not be obvious. After time it will all fit together perfectly.

Never give in to doubt about these eternal facts. This part you can know for sure.

> *"Who, being in very nature God, did not consider equality with God something to be used to his own advantage; rather, he made himself nothing by taking the very nature of a servant, being made in human likeness. And being found in appearance as a man, he humbled himself by becoming obedient to death— even death on a cross! Therefore God exalted him to the highest place and gave him the name that is above every name, that at the name of Jesus every knee should bow, in heaven and on earth and under the earth, and every tongue acknowledge that Jesus Christ is Lord, to the glory of God the Father."* (Philippians 2:6-16)

How much of God's grand plan for my life do I have clearly in focus? How much effort have I invested in complicating the issues?

55
Focussing your Vision

One of the most frequently book marked verses in an online version of the Bible is Jeremiah 29:11. Countless thousands have taken comfort there. But too few have considered the whole context for this gem. We touched upon it earlier but we need to drill down some.

Here is the story. This book marked verse is from a letter Jeremiah wrote from Jerusalem to Babylon to the exiles there. They were in captivity 800 km from home as the crow flies. They couldn't have their homeland or their inherent desires.

> *"This is what the LORD Almighty, the God of Israel, says to all those I carried into exile from Jerusalem to Babylon: 'Build houses and settle down; plant gardens and eat what they produce. Marry and have sons and daughters; find wives for your sons and give your daughters in marriage, so that they too may have sons and daughters. Increase in number there; do not decrease. Also, seek the peace and prosperity of the city to which I have carried you into exile. Pray to the LORD for it, because if it prospers, you too will prosper.'"*
> *(Jeremiah 29:4-7)*

"Folks, this place sucks; it isn't what you wanted; it isn't what you expected. This is what you must do. Fix the house and make it better than the next one as an example. Plant a garden and make your own way. You aren't a victim. You are here. This is home for a while. Well, actually a long while. Raise your kids and get them established so they can in turn get their kids properly raised. And while you are at it, get involved in the community. Make it a better place with your prayers and your participation."

"You have seventy years here and you must make it a good time. While you are here don't watch the motivational speakers on Babylon TV. They lie; they deceive. You are going to have to block that channel."

> *"This is what the LORD says: 'When seventy years are completed for Babylon, I will come to you and fulfill my good promise to bring you back to this place.'"* *(Jeremiah 29:10)*

"Hey folks, after seventy years you get to go home to Jerusalem. You have got to love that!"

Do you see what God was saying? Your life is here. You are the seed. You must bloom where you are planted. Don't lose heart. God sees way farther down the road than your headlights could ever reach. In fact, you might not even live to see the fulfillment of the plan. It may be played out in the next generation. But it is none the less God's plan for you. Your zipline extends far beyond the final landing platform.

This story in Jeremiah is a specific set of instructions to a limited group of exiles but it shows us how God works. And because He is the same today, we can be sure God has a master plan for you too. This long-term plan isn't about leaving Babylon; it is about being the best you can be in Babylon for now. Later is another matter and it will come.

> *"'For I know the plans I have for you,' declares the LORD, 'plans to prosper you and not to harm you, plans to give you hope and a future.'"*
> *(Jeremiah 29:11)*

God has this figured out for you too! Eventually the Babylon chapter will close. But maybe not even in your lifetime. Then again, maybe. God knows. Nobody else does. And you are not able to redesign it no matter how hard you fight the plan. If you are smart you will just get on board and ride this moment to the full.

When you get it right this is the heritage you will create.

> *"'Then you will call on me and come and pray to me, and I will listen to you. You will seek me and find me when you seek me with all your heart. I will be found by you,' declares the LORD, 'and will bring you back from captivity. I will gather you from all the nations and places where I have banished you,' declares the LORD, 'and will bring you back to the place from which I carried you into exile.'"* *(Jeremiah 29:12-14)*

The old Gospel tract, used to impact millions started with Law #1, "God loves you and has a wonderful plan for your life." It is true. Sadly, most people invest little time uncovering that plan. Without question, it is opaque. You cannot guess it out moving forward. You can only trace it out looking back.

You must learn to see with the eye of faith that which is unseeable by your regular faculties. And when you get that big long term view firmly planted in your soul you will find a deep sense of awe. When you see what God sees and focus on it, it is awesome!

> *Who can help me keep my eye on the big picture?*
> *Who can I help develop a better vision for life?*

56
Yelling Cowabunga!

There are defining moments when courage rises up within us and the peace of God prompts us to take a bold step of faith. It's an intelligent risk. The sum of our calculations indicated that the Lord of Adventure is trustworthy.

We jump into the unknown. It's exhilarating. Then almost immediately, the temptation to second guess our choice is before us. "What have I done?" "It would have been better to die in Egypt than in the desert." How quickly we forget how dreary and grey Egypt was.

You are in transition. If you're a 90s Generation X'er, let a "cowabunga" roll out of your vocal chords. If you love driving in the Outback, then scream "aieeee." Throw caution to the wind of the Holy Spirit.

Listen to the passionate words of Paul,

> *"Brothers, I do not consider myself yet to have taken hold of it. But one thing I do: Forgetting what is behind and straining toward what is ahead, I press on toward the goal to win the prize for which God has called me heavenward in Christ Jesus." (Philippians 3:13-14)*

May you also transition with that kind of resolve—this one thing I do! Live in the present knowing that your future is in God's good hands.

"Ladies and gentlemen. Please welcome Mr. Bruce Cockburn as he leaves us with a song to carry us forward with passion and fire for the rest of our journeys."

> "Lord of the starfields
> Ancient of Days
> Universe Maker
> Here's a song in your praise
> Wings of the storm cloud
> Beginning and end
> You make my heart leap
> Like a banner in the wind
> O love that fires the sun
> Keep me burning.

Lord of the starfields
Sower of life,
Heaven and earth are
Full of your light
Voice of the nova
Smile of the dew
All of our yearning
Only comes home to you
O love that fires the sun
keep me burning"

Did you catch the earlier sentence? This isn't about throwing caution to the winds of time; it is about throwing caution to the wind of the Holy Spirit.

The Holy Spirit is not just a force. The Holy Spirit is God and He (never "it") is personally more than willing to give you the confidence and comfort you need for a wonderful ride. Yes it takes perspective, obedience, a clean heart and a prepared mind.

The breeze in your face; the beauty of nature whizzing by; the gentle whirring of the well lubricated pulleys; the secure grip of the harness. You are on the zipline! Yes, in a blink the ride will end. That is then; this is now!

What is that breeze? Where is the awe? Conquering fear. Release from guilt. Overwhelming love for God. Stirring love for others. Purpose for life. Compassion for the needy. Endurance for the tough stuff. Peace beyond measure. The freedom to forgive. The desire to reach and help people. The comfort of togetherness with like-minded people. Leaving your beautiful mark as a legacy. Rising respect from others. Wisdom to spread far and wide. Calm assurance of the better zipline to come. Knowing God!

Who would ever want to reach the final platform? One ride leads to another. It just gets more interesting as you get used to the equipment, the pace, the pauses and the thrills on your zipline.

You get it! It is awesome!

And, oh my! What a ride!

Cowabungaaaaaaaaaaaaaaaaaa!!!!!!!!!!!!!!!!!!

Now what?

Appendix A
Values

The following are a list of possible things to value. Simply put, a value is something you believe is important to you and it shows itself in the way you live. These potential values are talked about in chapter 14. There is a brief exercise there to help you sort out your own thinking.

Achievement

Advancement at work

Adventure

Affection (love and caring)

Arts

Bible (knowledge and compliance)

Challenging problems

Change and variety

Church life

Close relationships

Competence

Competition

Cooperation

Country

Creativity

Decisiveness

Democracy

Ecological awareness

Economic security

Education

Effectiveness

Efficiency

Ethical practice

Family time

Friendships

Growth

Having a family

Helping society

Honesty

Independence

Influencing others

Inner harmony

Integrity

Intellectual status

Involvement

Job tranquility

Knowledge

Leadership

Location

Loyalty

Market position

Marriage

Meaningful work

Merit

Money

Open and honest relationships

Order (tranquility, stability, conformity)

Privacy

Public service

Purity

Quality involvements

Quality relationships

Recognition (respect from others, status)

Religion and faith
Reputation
Responsibility and accountability
Security
Self-respect
Serenity
Sophistication
Spirituality
Stability
Status
Supervising others
Time freedom
Truth
Vacation
Wealth
Wisdom
Working under pressure
Working with others
Working alone

Appendix B
Bible Passage Index

Compass Coaching International

The four authors of this book are the Board members of Compass Coaching International.

"I Need a Life Coach!"

Life Coaching is a new and rapidly growing profession. We have a list of competent and Certified Life Coaches eager to help you with the decisions you need to be making today. Our coaching affiliates are listed at www.compasscoaching.info.

"I Want to Be a Life Coach!"

We have designed a program to train Life Coaches who want to move their clients beyond just understanding their problems. Using a biblical paradigm of change that deals with heart issues and real life strategies, our curriculum delivers well tested tools to help people of all economic brackets live their lives to the fullest.

Life Coaching is a very fulfilling and rewarding profession. You can apply the training we give you to become an effective Life Coach. More than that we teach you how to create a Life Coaching practice. Depending on how you want to approach the Life Coaching dimension of your life, you may use the training to supplement your present life and ministry or you can turn it into a full time career. It is up to you. We teach you everything you need to know and point you to all the resources to make a full time income as a Life Coach if that is your desire.

Sometimes people take the course without intention to become a Life Coach but as a substitute for hiring a Life Coach. This gives two benefits. You will see how Life Coaching works from the inside and you will have sufficient intereaction with the trainers to receive personal coaching as well.

1. Learn More: Visit www.CompassCoachingInternational.com and www.CompassCoaching.info

2. Free Helps: Register at www.CompassCoachingInternational.com and find resources in the members area.

3. Personal Contact: Contact any of our Board members or Accredited Coaches by phone or email. We encourage those we accredit to offer the first conversation at no charge. This will help you determine if a particular Life Coach is a good fit for you. Contact information is on our websites.

Made in the USA
Charleston, SC
22 June 2011